Strategic Thinking

A Four Piece Puzzle

Bill Birnbaum

Douglas Mountain Publishing
Costa Mesa, CA

Strategic Thinking:
A Four Piece Puzzle
By Bill Birnbaum

Copyright © 2004 William S. Birnbaum
Published: January 2004
Second printing: August 2007

Published by
Douglas Mountain Publishing
1798 Oriole Drive,
PO Box 2216
Costa Mesa, CA 92628
Phone: 714-549-2990
Fax: 714-435-1157
Website: www.DouglasMountain.com

ISBN: 1-932632-13-1 / 978-1-932632-13-2

Publisher's Cataloging-In-Publication Data
(Prepared by The Donohue Group, Inc.)

Birnbaum, William S.
  Strategic thinking : a four piece puzzle / Bill Birnbaum.
    p. : ill. ; cm.
  ISBN: 1-932632-13-1
  Includes index.
1. Strategic planning. 2. Business planning. I. Title.
HD30.28 .B57 2004
658.4/012

Printed in the United States

Contents

About the Author

Bill Birnbaum, CMC, is President of Birnbaum Associates, Business Strategy Consultants. He helps management teams develop a clear vision for their future, and then turn that vision into a sound business strategy.

Since 1983, he has published and edited *Business Strategies Newsletter*, offering insights and ideas for strategic-minded leaders. He is the author of the book, *If Your Strategy is So Terrific, How Come it Doesn't Work?* (AMACOM, 1990). In 2000, he developed "Strategy 21™" a strategic planning process designed specifically to help business managers address the challenges of the 21st century.

Bill is a speaker for the American Management Association's strategy courses and also speaks frequently at association meetings. He addresses timely topics related to business strategy development and implementation.

He served on the board of directors for three high-growth corporations: Industrial Scientific Research Corp., Trans-Met Engineering Corp., and Woodroof Laboratories Inc. All three were acquired per the plan he helped them develop. He's certified as a Certified Management Consultant (CMC) by the Institute of Management Consultants. He holds a Bachelor's Degree in Electrical Engineering from The City College of New York, School of Engineering, and a Master's Degree in Business Administration from California State University – Fullerton.

Dedication

With love to my wife Wendy.
She's shared my excitement for this project,
and for everything else in my life.

And with love to my sons,
Larry and Doug.
Both are developing their own strategy
for their own life.
And I'm certainly proud of them.

Acknowledgments

While I'm the "official" author of this book, I'm hardly the only person responsible for its content. Therefore, I have many people to thank. I owe a special thanks to my friend and colleague, John Hall. For as my mentor throughout the writing process, John consistently "held my feet to the fire." When I committed to finishing a particular chapter by "a week from Friday," John actually wrote my commitment on his calendar. He looked so serious about it, I figured I'd better keep my promise to John.

Also, a special thanks to my editor, Tony Stubbs. Some months ago, I was so darn confident in my own writing, I figured I didn't need an editor. Tony taught me otherwise. He helped to make this a better book.

I'd also like to thank all of the men and women of the Professional Service Providers. They too were instrumental in holding my feet to the fire. And they helped me decide on a title for this book. As they can tell you, I found writing this book only a little bit more difficult than selecting among a handful of prospective titles.

And a thanks to my wife, Wendy. Most of the time, she just let me "do my own thing" writing chapter after chapter. Then, every once in a while, she'd review what I'd written and suggest some changes. She was ever so careful with her suggestions. I was ever so receptive to each of them. Well … to most of them.

Finally, I'd like to thank my clients. I'm grateful to all of them for all the thoughts, on all the issues, during all the hours, in all the strategy sessions, over all the years. Because of my clients, I've learned the vast majority of what you're about to read.

Introduction

What's the difference? Why are some business leaders successful at building strong, thriving enterprises while others continually flounder? Why do some consistently manage a healthy mixture of profit and growth while others prepare for their next layoff? Why do some firms radiate enthusiasm, commitment and fun while others leave hardly a memory?

For the last 24 years, I've searched for answers to these questions. During those years, I've worked in strategy sessions with teams of senior managers from client companies. And those strategy sessions were far from "just another meeting." Each was an intensive analysis of issues at the very heart of the organization. My clients wrestled with tough, open-ended questions. Questions such as …

Why do customers choose to buy our products or services? What might occur to change their mind about choosing our products or services? What can we do about preventing that?

What core competencies have led to our success? Are our competencies truly of competitive advantage? Are they impossible – or at least extremely difficult – for competitors to copy?

What are our "natural" constraints to growth? What's holding us back? What's the weakest link in our business model?

The client-companies I've worked with include organizations of every size – from Fortune 500s to entrepreneurial start-ups. They represent a variety of industries, including low, medium and high-tech manufacturing, and services, including financial, healthcare, law, communications, real estate development and consulting. When arriving at their strategy session, each team of managers enjoyed its own specific level of success. Some of their companies were healthy, thriving, profitable businesses, others thrashed about attempting to reverse their decline.

But large or small, fat or skinny, plain or fancy, all brought me closer to concluding why some build profitable, growing, fun-to-work-at enterprises ... and why others fail.

I've discovered that the more successful managers – and the more successful management teams – place more emphasis on strategic *thinking* than on strategic *planning*. Oh sure, they develop a strategic plan. And they publish that plan. And they share it with their employees. But their first priority is creating an environment of strategic thought. They then use strategic thinking in building a shared vision of their company's future. Finally, in deciding how they'll accomplish that vision, they use strategic thinking to develop their strategic plan.

I've also discovered that those successful managers – and successful management teams – focus on four fundamental factors, or four pieces of the strategic puzzle:

1. Rather than try to accomplish "everything," they diligently maintain *focus*.
2. They develop and maintain an intimate understanding of their *markets* and of their customers within those markets.
3. They truly care about – thus they nurture – their *people*.
4. And they carefully manage their *processes*.

Accordingly, I've arranged this book in four parts, each containing a number of chapters discussing important strategic concepts. In Part I, we'll discuss the first piece of the puzzle – *focus*. There, you'll learn that focus is one of my two strong biases. It's a point I drive home consistently with my clients. And it isn't enough to focus on just a few activities. You've also got to be sure they're the *right* activities.

In Part II, we'll discuss your *markets*. In our capitalistic economy, there's only one way to make money – you've got to sell something to somebody. So you and your management team had better care a whole lot about marketing. In Part II, we'll examine your marketplace, your product or service offering, and your relationship with your customer.

In Part III, we'll talk about leading your *people*. Remember I told you that one of my two strong biases is focus? Well, my other bias is this: It's one thing to develop a strategy; it's quite another to get the darn thing implemented. And you're not likely to implement it successfully if your employees don't care about it. So you'd better get your employees to care about your strategy. There's just one way to do that. You'd first better care about your employees.

In Part IV, we'll discuss managing *process*. Businesses contain processes and systems. And those processes and systems follow certain truisms, such as "diminishing returns," "the 80-20 rule," and "the path of least resistance." Also in this section, we'll contrast "working a process" with "working a project." And we'll explain when you can beneficially use each … and when you can't.

Please be sure to read both appendices. Appendix A discusses development of your mission statement. There, we'll answer three important questions: "What is a mission statement?" Why do we need one?" And "How should we write a mission statement?" In fact, we'll offer a proven technique for developing your mission statement with just a few people, or with many people, participating.

In Appendix B, we'll talk about reinventing the strategic planning process. There, we'll explain why it's time to reinvent the process and we'll offer a new planning model – a model more appropriate to the realities of our 21st century.

Over the years, many have suggested that I write a book about these strategic lessons I've learned. And for years, I responded to those suggestions by saying, "I'm too busy." But, over time, I came to realize that, through such a book, I could help far more managers and management teams than I could through my consulting and teaching alone. And so, I found the time to write the book you now hold.

Much of my work on this book I did during "off hours." And in odd places – hotel rooms, airports, sort of "here, there and everywhere." In fact, as I write these very words, I'm seated (not terribly comfortably) aboard a nighttime flight from Atlanta, Georgia to Orange County, California.

I hope you will gain from this book. That the truths about business strategy I've discovered over the last two and a half decades will help you improve your business. I hope my messages will help you to lead your management team. To steepen your growth curve. To brighten your profit picture. Toward these objectives, I've written this book.

Bill Birnbaum, CMC

PART I

FOCUS

CHAPTER 1

THE LAW OF THINGS

As a 22-year-old electronics engineer, fresh out of college, I landed a job with Beckman Instruments in Fullerton, California. There, I had the good fortune to work for the Chief of Electrical Engineering, a fellow named Tony Del Duca.

Tony was a born teacher and, from him, I learned quite a bit about engineering. More importantly though, he was also something of a philosopher and enjoyed teaching lessons about life. From time to time, he'd instruct me, an impressionable young man, about such diverse subjects as politics, career development, playing the stock market, fine dining and dating girls.

Without doubt, the most universally applicable of Tony's lessons, was "The Law of Things." Most would refer to the diagram which Tony drew on the blackboard as "The Bell-shaped Curve." It's familiar to all who've ever sat through a course on statistics or probability.

Tony explained it like this ...

On a scale of 0 to 10, most neckties cost about 5. Sure you can buy some very fine hand-sewn, silk neckties at a price that would score a 9 or 10. And you can score a 0 or 1 by shopping for a necktie in a discount department store. But if you took all the prices of all the neckties for sale, and ranked them on a scale of 0 to 10, you'd find their prices clustered around 5.

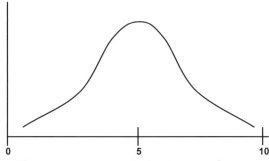

Figure 1 - 1: The Bell-shaped Curve

And on a scale of 0 to 10, the height of most adult American males would score about 5. Sure, each of the Boston Celtics scores a 9 or more, and jockeys score 0 or 1. But on a scale of 0 to 10, the majority of American men center around 5.

The price of neckties and the height of adult American males have one thing in common. Both cluster around the middle, with only a very few either very low or very high.

This "bell-shaped curve" is a natural phenomenon. It applies with such frequency that it's called the "normal distribution." It works not only for neckties and the Boston Celtics, but also for the acceleration of automobiles, the time required to shine your shoes, and the annual rainfall in your home town. In fact, applications of the bell-shaped curve are so numerous that it's only a slight exaggeration to call it, as Tony did, "The Law of Things."

And the bell-shaped curve applies, in many ways, in the world of business. Consider an activity for which your organization might compare itself against its competitors. Take marketing, for example. A few firms are excellent at marketing. IBM comes to mind immediately. IBM scores a 9 or 10 in marketing. And some companies are terrible at marketing – like many of those that go broke each year. They score a 0 or 1.

Most firms, however, are just about as good at marketing as a whole bunch of their competitors. On a scale of 0 to 10, they score about 4, 5 or 6. Here, too, the bell-shaped curve works.

It also works for cost of manufacturing, for product development and for financial strength. For each of those factors, almost everyone in the industry falls near the middle of the curve – about 4, 5 or 6 – while a few score very high and a few score very low.

You'll find that the bell-shaped curve is particularly useful when considering your company's strengths and weaknesses because it helps you view those strengths and weaknesses *in comparison to your competition*. And that's important. It isn't enough to say, "We're good at marketing." You must be able to say, "We're significantly better at marketing than are our competitors." For only then could you build a strategy based on a significant competitive advantage.

Think about each suggested strength and weakness in comparison to your competitors. How do you score? Right there in the middle of the pack – a 4, 5, or 6 with all the rest? Or do you score a 0, 1, or 2? In financial management perhaps? If you do score a 0, 1, or 2, you've just identified a *competitive weakness*— something you can work to correct (see Figure 1 - 2).

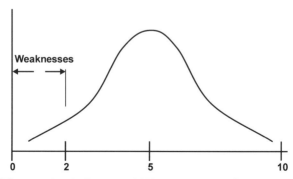

Figure 1 - 2: Internal Weaknesses Score 0 to 2

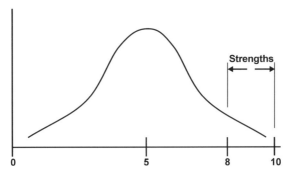

Figure 1 - 3: Internal Strengths Score 8 to 10

Go on to score the next issue. Marketing, perhaps. How do you score? About 8 or 9? Good. You've identified a *competitive strength*. Your challenge, as we'll soon see, will be to build a strategy based on that competitive strength (see Figure 1 - 3).

You'll discover that, as compared to your competition, most of the skills, activities and assets of your organization are neither strengths nor weaknesses. In most areas, your company is "in the middle of the pack." This means that your list of strengths and your list weaknesses will both be relatively short. That's great! For short lists lead to focus.

An interesting example of an organization building on internal strengths comes from a client of ours – a small electronics manufacturer on the West Coast. The company, formed by two talented engineers, works in the field of process instrumentation. The company is very good at going out into the factories of the nation, finding out what a particular process is all about, identifying specific measurement problems, wrapping its arms around those problems, and inventing customized solutions. So this little company focuses on those tougher problems, such as problems in harsh environments – hot, dusty, corrosive, and, at times, explosive environments. This little company has managed to carve out a nice little niche for itself in an otherwise very competitive marketplace.

Use the bell-shaped curve to identify your company's strengths and weaknesses as compared to your competition. Then be sure the strategies you develop build on your strengths and correct your weaknesses.

Key Success Factors

When you meet to "talk strategy" with your management team, your conversation might include a wide variety of topics. But rather than go for variety, you should focus. Focus on the issues key to the success of your organization. But how to discover those key issues? How to identify those activities most critical to the success of your company?

Here's how ...

On the first morning of your strategy session, ask your planning team an important question. On a flip-chart easel, write ...

> **For our organization to be successful, we *must*
> be especially good at the following activities:**
> **1.**
> **2.**
> **3.**

Then, challenge your team to provide two or three answers (but no more) to that question.

Ask everyone in the room to first spend a few moments thinking about the question and writing their answers individually. Then, have each person read their own answers aloud. Next, discuss any differences of opinion, and finally, arrive at a consensus. Record your final answers on a flip-chart easel and entitle the list "Key Success Factors."

This exercise, requiring about an hour and a half or so, provides a short list of "activities you've got to be good at." That's most important. For following the development of your Key Success Factors, you'll want to develop your lists of internal strengths and internal weaknesses. And when listing those internal strengths and weaknesses, you'll certainly include some very important factors. But you'll also need to avoid listing some very *un*important factors. So test each suggested strength or weakness by asking, "Does this suggested strength or weakness directly relate to one of our Key Success Factors?" If your answer is "no," then cross out the suggested strength or weakness.

As the manager for one of Hewlett Packard's Colorado divisions once put it, "We don't want to spend our valuable time discussing the color of the stripes in the parking lot." He's right. You'll want to use your time focusing on those factors most important to your success – your Key Success Factors.

And it's important to limit your list of Key Success Factors to two, or at most three. Here's why ...

In creating a list of "things we've got to be good at," management teams frequently include six or eight factors. Typically, they'll list, "understanding the customer," "producing a low-cost product," "managing expenses," "hiring good people," and "developing innovative marketing programs."

The lists are certainly complete. Too complete! They're so all-inclusive, they're not much more than "apple pie and motherhood." And they certainly don't imply focus.

But focus is exactly what's required for success. Focus on a few things, on the most important things, on two or three (but no more) key success factors. In any business, two or three activities are the primary determinants of success. If the firm's management team is very good at those activities, and just mediocre at everything else, the company will be successful. Yes, you read it right, it's OK to be *just mediocre at everything else.*

For example ...

In the real estate development industry, land acquisition and cash management are the two key success factors. If every other factor concerning the business of the development company were just average, but the company were excellent at acquiring well-located, easily developable land, and the firm were also excellent at maintaining liquidity, the company would do well. Not that the developer shouldn't attempt to deliver a well-constructed product with good financing. He should. But nothing is a greater determinant of success than having, or not having, the right piece of land, and remaining in a cash-liquid position.

In the computer software market, the key success factors are establishing efficient channels of distribution and providing after-sales support. Too much concern about writing "efficient code" may be a technical nicety, but from a competitive point of view, it's a waste of resources.

In the strategy consulting business, the key success factors are communicating with executive decision-makers and helping management teams think more deeply about their enterprise than they *ever* have before. For strategy consultants, too much concern about publishing attractive reports is focusing on the wrong thing.

Help your management team discover the Key Success Factors for your business. Then make sure you're very good at those specific activities. And don't spend a lot of energy becoming excellent at activities that are not as important.

The Question Mark

My two sons, Larry and Doug, are grown now. When they were young boys, they learned about the world around them by asking, "Why, dad?" And, from them, I learned, too. For the boys taught me the value of the question mark. Without ever realizing it, Larry and Doug convinced me that the question mark is especially valuable to a child, an adult, a consultant, and a business manager. In fact, the most useful tool in the business world isn't the computer. It isn't even the cellular telephone or the personal digital assistant. It's the question mark.

The question mark is particularly useful when you need to find things out. To get to the reason. To identify the real problem hidden behind a whole bunch of symptoms. Like this ...

Mr. A.: "What's the problem?"

Mr. B.: "Our sales have really fallen off."

Mr. A. "How come?"

Mr. B.: "Our sales force has become terribly ineffective in selling our products in our traditional market."

Mr. A.: "Why?"

Mr. B.: "It seems our customers are preferring, more and more, to buy our competitors' products."

Mr. A.: "Why is that?"

Mr. B.: "Because our competitors have been coming out with one new product after another."

Mr. A.: "Haven't you been doing the same?"

Mr. B.: "No, our product line is pretty mature. In fact, a number of our products are actually obsolete."

Mr. A.: "How come?"

Mr. B.: "Consciously or unconsciously, we've been taking a short-term view of our business. Milking our old product line and falling farther and farther behind our competitors' product offerings. I guess we're now paying for our earlier short-term thinking."

Bingo! We just got a handle on the fundamental problem.

You know, it's amazing how much we can learn by simply asking, "Why?" Try it. Go into your planning sessions a bit suspicious – suspicious that the "weaknesses" as initially expressed, aren't fundamental weaknesses, but rather *symptoms* of weaknesses. Before solving any problem, you'll need to discover the fundamental weaknesses lying behind the symptoms. Keep asking "why?"

Thank you, Larry and Doug.

Thinking Strategically

You'll need to be sure that your management team is thinking strategically. But just what is strategic thinking? It's a top-down, "big picture" view of your entire organization. It's based on a deep understanding of your business.

Strategic thinking isn't about detailed tactics. While thinking strategically, you won't become concerned with the tactical problem that machine number three on line number four breaks down every week or so. Rather, strategic thinking will lead you to consider the needs of your customer, the benefits you offer that customer, and the reason your customer buys your products or services.

In thinking strategically, you'll be concerned with doing the right things, rather than doing things right. This distinction is important. Shortly before he died in 1984, the famous photographer Ansel Adams spoke at Orange Coast College in Costa Mesa, California. During his talk, Adams made a very interesting point, one that helps us to understand this difference between strategic thinking and tactical thinking. Adams said, "There is nothing worse than a sharp picture of a fuzzy concept." Clearly, strategy must precede tactics. Strategic thinking must precede tactical thinking.

Management guru Peter Drucker makes the same point when he says, "There is nothing more wasteful than becoming highly efficient at doing the wrong thing." Indeed, you use strategic thinking in deciding *what* to do. You use tactical thinking in deciding *how* to do it.

Unfortunately, most managers are predisposed to think tactically rather than strategically. This is for a number of reasons. First, they're trained to do so. Most educational programs teach highly specific disciplines – financial accounting, sales management, digital design, quality assurance. You name it. A very small percentage of our total educational experience aims at the more global "big picture."

Another reason why managers tend to think tactically rather than strategically is that most managers have a very specific functional responsibility – sales, marketing, accounting, human resources, manufacturing, product design, customer service. Few have "big picture" responsibility. But even those with "big picture" responsibility likely have spent much of their career working in one specific functional discipline or another, so they tend to "see the world" from a specific point of view, much as they did earlier in their career.

Yet one more reason why most managers tend not to think strategically is that their day-to-day responsibilities call for them to deal with tactics. They're "down in the trenches" executing a step at a time. Not very often are they called upon to think strategically. In most organizations, not often enough. In fact, in most organizations, just once a year – at some off-site strategic planning session – are a small number of high-level executives challenged to think strategically about their enterprise. Too few people; too infrequently.

Why it's important to think strategically

Strategic thinking is now more important than ever before. Success today calls for a far greater level of strategic thinking than it did just a decade ago. In fact, here in our 21st century, strategic thinking has become a prerequisite to success. As we've come through the 1990s, we've seen the business environment become far "tougher" and far less forgiving of mediocrity.

Here in our 21st century, we operate in a new economic reality, a reality characterized by rapid change. Change in information technology, in networked organizations, in knowledge workers "carrying the business around in their heads," and in globalization – globalization in three dimensions:

1. Products and services being sold wherever income is higher
2. Production moving to wherever labor costs are lower
3. Labor moving to wherever wages are higher.

In suggesting that organizations need to think more strategically, I don't mean to suggest they need to think strategically as a once-a-year event. Rather they need to think strategically as an on-going process. Indeed, strategic thinking must become a way of life for any organization wishing to thrive – indeed to survive – in our 21st century. For the "chaos" of our 21st century is continuous. It isn't waiting patiently for your next "planning cycle." If your management team isn't constantly (or at least, frequently) thinking strategically, your organization is highly vulnerable.

How Does Strategic Thinking Differ from Strategic Planning?

When I speak at association meetings, attendees often ask me, "Is strategic thinking the same thing as strategic planning?" And it's a logical question for after all, the two are related. But they're not exactly the same. Strategic planning is a highly structured process. Its tangible output is a written document – the strategic plan – containing a set of well-quantified objectives and a number of strategies designed to accomplish those objectives. And the strategic plan has a "life span" of a specific number of years, typically, three, five, or ten.

Strategic thinking is different. For one, it's generally less structured. While its output will often contain a set of written notes, those notes are generally far less formal than a strategic plan. And the resultant notes aren't necessarily intended to apply for a specific number of years. In fact, the writing of notes is actually of secondary importance. *The most important benefit of strategic thinking is the resultant strategic vision shared among your management team.* This shared strategic vision must be based on your management team's deep understanding of the business. The management team's strategic thought, its shared vision, and its deep understanding of the business, empower your organization in its competitive environment.

CHAPTER 2

THE SW-OT MATRIX™

It's something of an exaggeration to say that "everyone is familiar with SWOT." But it isn't *much* of an exaggeration. Indeed, most business managers know that SWOT stands for strengths, weaknesses, opportunities and threats. An analysis of the company's current situation, the SWOT, or "situation analysis," provides a look at both the internal and external aspects of the organization. And in looking both internally and externally during the SWOT analysis, you and your management team will itemize both the good and bad news – that is, you'll list:

- Internal good news (strengths)
- Internal bad news (weaknesses)
- External good news (opportunities), and
- External bad news (threats).

Simple, right? Well no, not really. You see, many – in fact, most – management teams hurriedly develop lists of strengths, weaknesses, opportunities and threats that are far too long.

Don't do that! Instead be sure that your management team keeps your lists focused on the few most significant of your strengths, your weaknesses, your opportunities and your threats. The good news is that you've got the tools to keep your lists short and well-focused. Yes, we've discussed them all in Chapter 1. The Key Success Factors, the Bell-shaped Curve, and the Question Mark, will all help you and your team stay focused on those strengths and weaknesses that are truly significant.

Remember? You'll use your list of Key Success Factors to test any suggested internal strength or internal weakness. You'll ask, "Does this suggested strength or weakness directly relate to one of our Key Success Factors?" If the answer is "yes," the suggested strength or weakness has passed the first necessary test.

Next, on the bell-shaped curve, a suggested strength must score an 8, 9, or 10 as compared to your competitors. And a suggested weakness must score a 0, 1 or 2, as compared to your competitors.

Also, a suggested internal weakness must pass yet one more test. For very often, managers identify not fundamental weaknesses, but rather *symptoms* of weaknesses. You'll have to recognize any symptom as such, dig down beneath the symptom, and find the fundamental weakness which caused the symptom. How do you do that? By asking questions. Specifically, you ask the question, "Why?" Remember? The question mark is the business manager's most useful tool. And so, while discussing your internal weaknesses, be watchful of a symptom disguised as a weakness. Keep asking, "Why?" until you've uncovered the fundamental weakness hidden behind the symptoms.

After having completed your (short) lists of internal strengths and internal weaknesses, you'll be ready to move on to itemizing your external opportunities and external threats.

Here again, too many managers create long, unfocused lists. Again, resist that temptation! Stay focused.

Identifying Your Opportunities and Threats

You might ask, "Where should we look for opportunities and threats?" First look in a world called the macro-environment. This is a big, broad place. It's the world at large – all things that somehow *relate* to your organization. (See Figure 2 - 1.)

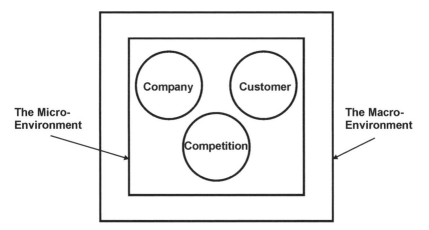

Figure 2 - 1: The Macro- and Micro-Environments

Issues in the macro-environment are not specific to your company. They're not even specific to your industry. But you care about them because they affect your business. They include economic conditions, for example. Economic conditions are not specific to any one industry. Rather, economic conditions impact all firms. The economy, then, is a macro-environmental issue.

Government regulations and politics, likewise. And consumer attitudes. Generally not specific to any particular industry. Demographic data – people moving into or out of regional areas. The aging of the population. Women's changing role in the workforce. Again, not industry specific. These issues impact all industries. They are macro-environmental factors.

Remember this word – "SPEELT." No, that's not a breakfast cereal; it's a word I made up to help us remember the various aspects of the macro-environment. SPEELT stands for:

- Societal
- Political
- Economic
- Environmental
- Legal
- Technological.

In thinking about the macro-environmental factors that affect your business, you'll need to consider each of these areas. And remember this, too: For the foreseeable future, our economy – in fact, our society – will continue to be impacted by two significant trends:

- Globalization, and
- Technology

Make sure you give strong consideration to both during your discussions of the macro-environment.

After looking at the macro-environmental factors, you'll next consider your micro-environment – the world that's a whole lot closer to home. It's the world in which your organization, its customers, its suppliers, its labor force and its competitors all interact. It's the industry and the marketplace in which you participate.

The micro-environment includes the segments of the marketplace to which your customers belong. It includes the reasons why your customers buy your products or services. The reasons why some of your prospective customers *don't* buy your products or services. Supplier relationships, your labor market – these are micro-environmental factors, all specific to your industry.

No look at the external environment is complete without an analysis of your competition. The competitive analysis includes an examination of the market segments served by both your firm and your competitors. Your market share versus theirs, and marketing mix, including product and service quality, pricing and distribution. A look at their position in the marketplace as compared to yours. And an examination of competitor *strengths* and *weaknesses.*

Competitor strengths and weaknesses are an important element in your situation analysis because a competitor strength translates into an *external threat* for your company. And a competitor weakness translates into an *external opportunity* for your company.

In itemizing your external opportunities, be careful, for in attempting to list external opportunities, many management teams mistakenly include a strategy or two. And it's no surprise, for opportunities and strategies are easily confused. Remember this: An opportunity is a *favorable external circumstance* which you might choose to pursue. But since it's external, the opportunity is *absolutely independent* of the existence of your organization.

And since the opportunity is independent of your firm's existence, it describes *no action* by your firm. So opportunity statements should have no action verbs. They shouldn't say, "Let's spin off into the foreign commercial market." Or, "Let's develop a new product line for the mid-price market." In those cases, you're really writing strategies.

If you recognize a "market demand in the foreign commercial market," then simply write your opportunity statement saying exactly that. Sure, you'll also develop strategies. But you'll develop strategies at a later step in the planning process. During the Situation Analysis, you're developing only four lists: Internal Strengths, Internal Weaknesses, External Opportunities and External Threats.

Okay, let's assume you've done a fine job in developing your situation analysis. But now what? Having developed your Situation Analysis, how in the heck can these resultant four lists (strengths, weaknesses, opportunities and threats) help you and your management team to develop a viable business strategy?

Great question. Glad you asked. Next, look on the walls of your conference room. Likely they're covered with large sheets of paper. And those sheets of paper contain statements – lots of them.

The first of those sheets reads, "These are our internal strengths." Next, internal weaknesses. Then, external opportunities. And finally, external threats. Actually, it's somewhat intimidating to walk into the conference room, look at all the statements you earlier developed, and think, "All we have to do now is to develop strategies." The danger, of course, is the very real possibility that your team will attempt to talk about all possible subjects at the same time. (Ever been to a meeting like that?)

Using the SW-OT Matrix™ to Develop Strategies

What you need is a tool. A tool you can use to pull one issue at a time down from the walls of the room, so that you can discuss a single issue at a time rather than try to discuss all issues at the same time.

A tool useful for this application is the SW-OT Matrix™. First, I'll apologize for never having thought of a pretty name for the SW-OT Matrix™. But, pretty name or not, SW-OT Matrix™ tells the story. Because SW-OT stands for strengths, weaknesses, opportunities and threats, and Matrix suggests that you're going to arrange items in a grid and look for relationships among those factors.

To develop the SW-OT Matrix™, you'll list your internal factors – strengths and weaknesses – in one dimension, and your external factors – opportunities and threats – in the other. And then you'll look for particular relationships between those internal and external factors. (See Figure 2 - 2.)

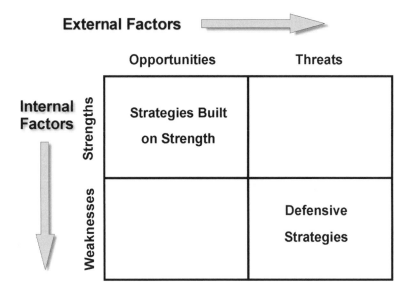

Figure 2 - 2: The SW–OT Matrix[TM]

Recall you have a list of external threats on the wall of your conference room. Look at each of those threats individually and ask, "When are we especially vulnerable to that particular threat?" Aren't you most vulnerable to a particular threat when you have one or more internal weakness which relates to that threat? Sure, that makes sense.

Here's an idea: How about starting another sheet of paper? And on the top of that sheet, write "Defensive Strategies." Then list your first external threat. Perhaps that first threat reads, "Our major competitor is going off-shore for low-cost production." Having listed that threat, you'll next consider which of your internal weaknesses align with that specific threat, thus making you especially vulnerable. (See Figure 2 - 3.)

Defensive Strategies

External Threat:

**Corresponding
Internal Weaknesses:**

Strategy:

Figure 2 - 3: Defensive Strategies

On that same piece of paper, you'll then list those *correspond-ing* internal weaknesses. Perhaps internal weakness # 2 reads: "We have obsolete factory equipment making our production costs high." Yes, that weakness does correspond to the low-cost com-petitor threat. Internal weakness # 3 might mention your poor balance sheet. If so, then it, too, relates to the specific threat, for a poor balance sheet would prohibit the capital investment re-quired to reduce manufacturing costs.

After having identified all the internal weaknesses that relate to the external threat you're then considering, write the word: "Strategy." Then consider, "What are we going to do about this particular threat combined with its corresponding weaknesses?

How will we deal with this situation? What is our strategy?" You won't forget all of the statements on all of the lists, on all of the sheets, covering the walls of your conference room. You'll use that information as backdrop to your strategy discussions. But you'll focus your team's attention on the subject at hand – on the relationship between the external threat you're then considering and its related internal weaknesses. In this manner, you'll deal with one external threat at a time. Then another. Then another.

You will thus continue to develop defensive strategies for each of your external threats, one at a time, until you've exhausted your list of external threats. If you earlier identified four external threats, you'll have four defensive strategic discussions. And each discussion will lead to a defensive strategy or to a set of defensive strategies.

Strategies Built on Strength

Then, you can turn your attention toward the brighter side of the coin. Recall that during your situation analysis, you identified a number of external opportunities. But are those opportunities really ones you should seriously consider? They are if – and only if – you possess the internal strengths that are both necessary and sufficient to "go get" those opportunities.

Start with a new sheet of paper. And on top of that paper, write "Strategies Built on Strength." (See Figure 2 - 4.) Next, list the first of the opportunities you listed during your Situation Analysis. Perhaps that opportunity reads, "Emerging market demand for a portable moisture monitor with an improved time constant." (Note: If you're in the banking business, your first opportunity is likely to be somewhat different from this example.)

Next, which of your internal strengths correspond to that external opportunity? Well, let's see – internal strength # 2 reads:

> # Strategies Built
> # On Strength
>
> **External Opportunity:**
>
>
> **Corresponding
> Internal Strengths:**
>
>
> **Strategy:**

Figure 2 - 4: Strategies Built on Strength

"We have a sales force in place in the market area where that opportunity exists." Strength # 4 reads: "We have additional capacity in R&D to develop the new product." See the point? You're aligning the particular opportunity with its corresponding internal strengths.

Now just before you develop a strategy to "go get" the opportunity, ask one very important question: "Are those corresponding internal strengths both *necessary and sufficient* to take advantage of this opportunity?" That is, do you have the necessary strengths to "win"?

If your answer to that most important question is "yes," next ask, "What is our strategy to pursue the opportunity?"

Next consider your second external opportunity, list its corresponding strengths, then develop your strategy. Then consider the third opportunity. Then the fourth. You'll continue developing strategies, building on strengths, until you've exhausted your list of external opportunities.

When I lecture on the SW-OT Matrix™, managers often ask, "What about the other two boxes in the model?" Might not an external threat align with some internal strengths? Or an external opportunity with some internal weaknesses? Good question.

Beyond the SW-OT Matrix™

Clearly there are some issues that will not fall neatly into either of the two boxes we've discussed, but will instead fall into one of the other two boxes. Or they'll fall outside the model entirely. Let me give you some examples from our experience in working with clients.

First, let's look at an example of an issue that fell into the threats – strengths category (the upper right corner of the SW-OT Matrix™). Some years ago, the management team for one of our client companies was absolutely paranoid about the labor union's potential entry into their organization. The number one threat that came up during the company's situation analysis was: "Here comes the union!" OK. We put that threat first on the threat list – with very little discussion. But if you were to look around the organization, you'd find absolutely nothing that made the firm vulnerable to the union. Wages and salaries were in order. Working conditions were excellent. And when an occasional grievance came up, two guys "jumped" on it, making it go away within half an hour. The company was absolutely not vulnerable to the union.

Nonetheless, you could not go into a planning session with this management team without the union threat emerging early in the discussion. If you were to place this issue on the SW-OT Matrix™, you'd set it in the upper right – at the alignment of external threats and internal strengths.

On the defensive strategies sheet, we wrote: "Threat #1: potential entry of labor union." Then we looked at our list of internal weaknesses. We were looking for a match between one or more of those weaknesses and the union threat. But we couldn't find a single corresponding weakness. So for "corresponding weaknesses" we wrote "none specific." But the planning team still wanted to strategize about the union. And they did. They wrote four strategies to counter the union threat. Funny thing – all four strategies began with the word "continue." Thus the management team actually reaffirmed the fact that they had been implementing the right strategies to counter the union threat. And while the discussion landed in an unusual corner of the SW-OT Matrix™, the process worked just fine.

Killing a Bad Idea

Regarding opportunities aligned with weaknesses – the model's lower left box – let's consider another example. One of our clients manufactures electronic power supplies – very high quality power supplies at very low volume that are used in military, space and high-end industrial applications. Their production process includes much hand labor, much inspection, and little automation. Certainly, their products are expensive. While compiling their opportunities list, the planning team listed the demand for very large quantity, very low price power supplies – real cheapies – for household appliances. To me, this seemed an odd fit, and I remember thinking, "What in the world are we going to do with this opportunity?"

When we arrived at the "Strategies Built on Strength" portion of our discussions, we wrote the opportunity on a fresh sheet of paper. And we asked, "Which of our internal strengths would support our going after this opportunity?" We looked at the list of internal strengths. Nothing. We found not one single internal strength to support the company's pursuing this specific opportunity. This was a high quality, low quantity operation, yet the opportunity called for high quantity, low price. Just the opposite. An entirely different business, in fact.

After a twenty minute discussion about this "no match" situation, the team still seemed floundering in indecision. So I stepped up to the flip chart easel and drew a diagonal red line from corner to corner across the entire sheet of paper In effect, I crossed out the opportunity. Sure it was an opportunity. But an opportunity for someone else. Not for this particular company. I actually held my breath waiting to see if the management team would let me get away with this very strong recommendation to "kill it."

In fact, they did let me get away with it. For that diagonal red line had significant value to the organization. For three months prior to that meeting, the company's managers had been debating the merits of going after that "low end" business. Here, we developed a common vision regarding the opportunity's lack of fit, and agreed to "kill it."

Let's consider a case where our discussion might not land in any of the four quadrants of the SW-OT Matrix™. One of our client companies was outgrowing its office building. At their then-current growth rate, they'd have to move in about five years. Five years! Heck, that's not a strength, a weakness, an opportunity or a threat. But it is an issue. It's something we should talk about during our strategic planning meetings.

Someone in the organization, after all, should pay attention to this requirement. If they don't do something about it soon, before we knew it, we'd have only three years; then two. Then the company really would have a weakness. So we entered this issue as a note on our reminder list. And during our strategy sessions, we made sure to address it. Per the resultant strategy, the vice president and the production manager became the "facilities planning committee." Their strategy called for contacting local real estate agents to search for larger facilities.

Notice one thing about using the SW-OT Matrix™. If you develop long lists of strengths, weaknesses, opportunities and threats, you'll develop many strategies. Too many. You'll lose focus. A long list of bewildering "tactical" strategies will result. The solution? Simple. Develop short lists of strengths, weaknesses, opportunities and threats.

CHAPTER 3

HEY, DON'T SET SO MANY OBJECTIVES!

An important aspect of focus is setting just a very few objectives. Objectives, as you know, are the measurements you'll use to track your success. Most management teams establish objectives from time to time, especially as a part of their strategic planning process. But most management teams set too many objectives.

The problem with having too many objectives is that it causes lack of focus. As a client of ours once said, "If *everything* is important, then *nothing* is important." But while understanding this problem intellectually, management teams still find it compelling to develop longer lists of objectives.

During many strategy sessions, I've stood up and delivered "my little mini-speech" about the importance of focus. In that speech, I encourage the management team to set perhaps six or seven or eight objectives. But, at times, they set objectives numbering into the double digits.

I recall one occasion where a client insisted, in spite of my warnings, on setting thirteen objectives. Concerned about their losing focus because "*everything* was important," I suggested they prioritize those thirteen objectives. And they did. They made six of their objectives an "A" priority, three a "B" priority, and four a "C" priority.

You know what? By the second quarterly review – a short six months later – they'd abandoned their "C" priorities to focus largely on the "A" priorities. Also, they were giving just token attention to the "B" priorities. Fortunately, having earlier prioritized their objectives, they all agreed which would "drop off the plate."

One reason why management teams set too many objectives is that their business (as any business) has so many "things" to measure. And they all seem important. For managers want to know that each and every machine, during each and every shift, is operating optimally. This is understandable. But the statistics for each and every machine during each and every shift don't belong in the company's strategic plan. Instead, a composite number representative of overall factory efficiency might belong in the strategic plan.

Think of all the measurements which your management team currently tracks. You could organize those measurements into two "rooms" – a front room and a back room. In the front room, you'd have the very few, top level measurements – your strategic objectives. These measurements give your senior managers the "big picture" of your company's performance.

In the back room, you'd have the many, many more measurements that offer a more detailed picture of your company's operations. There in the back room, the managers might well track statistics for each and every machine during each and every shift.

Hey Look, It's a Camel Race!

Okay, so which few measurements find their way into the front room? Which few should you include in your strategic plan? I'll answer that question with a story. Some years ago, I met a fellow who participated in a camel race. Yep, mounted on a dromedary, he raced across Australia for a month or so. East to west, as I recall.

About now, you might be wondering what in the world a camel race has to do with setting objectives. Yes, yes, I'm getting to that. Just suppose that one of the people competing in this race was the president of a mid-sized corporation in the United States. Suppose further that while racing across Australia, he gets to wondering how things are going at his business back in the States.

Suppose further that this camel-racing president comes upon a station (that's a ranch in Australia). And as he rides up to the station, the lady of the house comes to the door to greet him. "G'day," she says, with a friendly smile.

"Hello," he replies. "Say, do you think it would be okay if I were to use your phone? I've got to call back to my company in the United States. I'd like to find out how things are going."

"Fine, I don't mind. But you'll make it short, won't you? For international calls are expensive out here in the bush. Could you keep your call to less than a minute?"

"Oh yes, I'll do that. No more than a minute. I promise."

And as the president walks up to the phone, and as he dials the phone number, he thinks about the few questions he'll ask during his up-coming telephone call – a call that is to last no more than one minute.

And there's the answer. The quantified objectives for your company are those about which your president would inquire during his one minute call from the station in the Australian outback.

The message from this story is clear. Keep your focus. Keep your objectives lists short. Make sure your objectives measure the most important "stuff."

Tracking the Pulse of the Business

This same philosophy of focus applies when communicating with your board of directors. Some years ago, prior to the company's acquisition by Sterling Drug Inc., I served on the Board of Directors of Woodroof Laboratories, Inc. We directors worked with the president to develop a one-page form for reporting on the company's progress at our board meetings. The form was quite effective in its intended purpose. Also, it helped the president and his management team focus on those activities crucial to success in the business.

The form we developed contained two types of measurements. First, the obvious ones you'd certainly expect: sales revenue, profitability and cash flow. These were the "score board" measurements telling us whether we were "winning" or "losing" financially.

Measurements of the second type were both far less obvious and far more telling. They "dug deeper," and gave us the "pulse of the business." They told us "what's working and what isn't?"

These measurements include:
- Percentage of sales revenue from core customers
- Percentage of sales revenue from new accounts
- Number of new accounts for the period
- Percent of sales from new products
- Gross margin for each product
- Manufacturing cost per unit for each product.

As you can see, these "Key Performance Indicators," as we called them, actually offer a feel for our strategy — a strategy to maintain established core accounts while developing new accounts, introduce new products, and manage gross margin through reduction in manufacturing cost.

Obviously, we developed these specific Key Performance Indicators to fit a manufacturing organization. But we (or you) could just as well develop a list of Key Performance Indicators appropriate to any other type of organization. For example, a restaurant might monitor:

- Number of guest checks (bills rung up at the cash register)
- Average sales revenue per guest check
- Percentage of sales revenue for each of the three day parts (breakfast, lunch, and dinner).

A professional service organization (consulting, accounting, law) might monitor (in addition to that all-important billings per professional):

- Percent of billings to established accounts
- Number of new accounts for the period
- Source of new accounts (referrals, seminars, publications, etc.).

The trick to establishing Key Performance Indicators is to decide "what matters most" in your business. In effect, decide on your strategy. Then develop a set of Key Performance Indicators to track progress against that strategy. Doing so is well worth the effort, for the benefits are significant: your management team firmly focused on your strategy, and effective communication at a strategic level both among your management team and with your board of directors.

Set Your Objectives in Three Steps

Some years ago, I received a call from a company president who was experiencing a particularly frustrating problem. Seems that each time his management team attempted to establish their objectives, they'd end up talking about a number of subjects, seemingly, "all at the same time." Sure enough, as I sat in on their objective setting meeting, I observed their plunge into this world of "conversational chaos."

The chaos came about because the team tried to discuss each objective in isolation. They began by suggesting a particular objective, deciding "yes" they'd like to adapt it, then quantifying that objective for each of the next five years. Only after quantifying that first objective would they then consider what their second objective might be. Indeed, this attempt to take one objective at a time all the way through "the numbers stage" is a guaranteed formula for chaos.

I suggested that the team set objectives in three steps:
1. Decide on the essence of all of the objectives, then
2. Decide on the formula for measurement of all of the objectives, then
3. Quantify each of the objectives.

Most importantly, I suggested that the team avoid discussing numbers (step 3) until deciding on the measurement system (step 2) for *all* of their objectives.

The reason I asked them to separate these steps is that once they (or anyone) begin talking about numbers, the group can – and generally will – get awfully bogged down. That's why their team's conversations fell into chaos. They simply went off on a tangent, arguing about the appropriateness of a particular number. And, while getting all wrapped up deciding what a particular number should be, they lost sight of the "big picture" –their overall set of objectives.

Here's an example of the process I recommended. In their first step, the team might decide that the essence of an objective should be profitability. Also, they'd like to measure sales volume. And product quality. Additionally, in the area of human resources, they'd like to measure absenteeism. OK, now they've got the "big picture" – the essence of their entire set of objectives.

The Essence of the Objectives:
- Profitability
- Sales volume
- Product quality
- Employee absenteeism.

On to step two. Here, the management team needs to decide how to measure each one. That is, what's the formula? Perhaps, after some discussion, the team would decide on the following set of formulas:

The Formulas for Measuring the Objectives:
- Annual profit as a percentage of sales
- Total annual sales in dollars
- Product quality expressed as total annual warrantee costs in dollars
- Absenteeism measured as a percentage of labor hours lost during the year.

The trick is to finish the first two steps (identify the essence and establish the measurement method) for the entire set of objectives before ever thinking about numbers. That way, you'll avoid getting "all wrapped up" in a discussion about numbers and losing sight of your overall set of objectives. Remember – once you begin talking about numbers, you're down in tactics and will have a difficult time returning to your entire set of objectives.

An analogy I like (warning, however, not everyone is comfortable with this analogy) is to consider the three steps as follows:

1. Who's the patient?
2. Where should we stick the thermometer?
3. How high should we expect the column of mercury to climb?

See, I told you. Not everyone is quite so comfortable with this analogy. Remember though, first figure out who *all* of your patients are. Then figure out where to stick the thermometer *in each*. Then – and only then – determine how high the column of mercury should climb for each.

Is It Worth It?

From time to time, you and your management team will consider setting an objective requiring a measurement that you don't currently make. For example, you might consider an objective that would indicate the level of employee satisfaction. Or customer satisfaction. Such objectives would require your developing a survey.

Should you find yourself considering an objective calling for making a new measurement, stop and ask your team, "Is it worth it? Is having this objective so important that we're willing to build a new measurement system to track its progress?"

I'm not implying that any particular objective isn't important. I'm simply suggesting that you and your team take a realistic look at the question, "Is it worth creating a measurement system to track the objective?"

Your answer may well be "yes," but your management team should understand that measuring the objective will require additional resources. Is it really worth it?

CHAPTER 4

WHAT ARE YOU DOING THAT'S DIFFERENT?

R ecently, I worked with a consumer goods manufacturer, help-ing the management team develop its long-range, strategic plan. While setting their quantified objectives, the planning team suggested that they'd like to shoot for a 10 percent annual growth in sales revenue.

Having earlier reviewed the company's sales history, I recalled that growth had, for some years, been consistently between 2 and 6 percent, so I asked the planning team, "What will you do that's different?"

While the team thought about an answer to my question, I stepped up to the flip-chart easel and drew the "hockey stick curve." That's a curve – shaped very much like a hockey stick – showing an "all of a sudden" improvement (see Figure 4 - 1). I explained that improvements such as sales growth from low single-digit to double-digit percentages generally don't happen because someone – or even *everyone* – does a better job at doing the same old thing. Such abrupt change comes from doing something *different.*

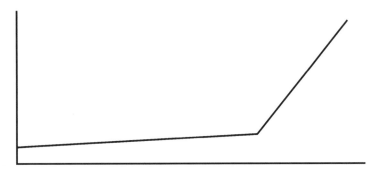

Figure 4 - 1: The Hockey Stick Curve

Again I asked the team, "What will you do that's different? What new and different strategy will you employ? In customer service? In marketing? In sales?"

After some time, the team confessed that they really hadn't thought about doing anything different. Rather, they just expected to work harder at doing the same thing they'd always done.

I suggested that they, therefore, should expect to see growth in the historic range of 2 to 6 percent. I based this expectation on two rules of thumb:

1. If you do what you've always done, you'll get what you've always gotten.
2. A sudden improvement from low single-digit to double-digit growth (represented by the hockey stick curve) comes from doing something different.

Yes, to improve significantly (in sales growth, for example), it's important to do something different than you were doing before. You've got to implement some significant change.

Doing Something Different Competitively

There's a second aspect to "doing something different." It's also important to do something different from your competitors.

Some years ago, a Southern California entrepreneur launched a business attempting to take "a few percentage points" of market share away from the industry leader. "Seems simple," he reasoned. "Since the leader has 65 percent of the market, he'd hardly miss only 3 to 5 percent. And that 3 to 5 percent should result in a nice little business for me."

Well, market leaders really *do* notice losses of "... only 3 to 5 percent." But keep reading. Things get worse.

The entrepreneur copied the leader; he developed a "me too" product and a "me too" marketing strategy. "To give the consumer a choice," he reasoned.

Result: Dismal performance. The company was soon drained of capital ... and energy. The company's investors quickly soured. Threats from lenders followed. And after a few strenuous years, an exhausted entrepreneur closed his business.

What was the problem?

The problem was that the entrepreneur's thinking was fundamentally wrong. He failed to adequately respect the industry leader. He underestimated how terribly difficult it is to take even a little bit of market share from the leader, particularly with a "me too" strategy. As is usually the case, the leader was firmly entrenched in the marketplace.

Solidly positioned in first place in the mind of customers, leaders enjoy a far greater "market awareness." Like IBM, Kleenex and Hertz, the leader's name comes to mind first when thinking of the product or service. Whether true or not, prospective customers generally assume the market leader offers better products and services than its smaller-share competitors. And when the customer is forced to choose among competing products or services he doesn't fully understand, the leader's brand provides the "safe" decision. Thus the powerful position of IBM in office automation, Kleenex in facial tissue, and Hertz in rental cars.

The leader's entrenchment is indeed firm. Leaders are tough to beat. The rich get richer. Faced with such formidable competition, what is the smaller or newer entrant to do? Must he simply stay out of the market? Or is there a way in?

Sure there's a way in. But the way in isn't to copy the leader's marketing strategy. The way in is to *do something different.* But different *how*?

Three choices – differentiate product or service, focus on a specific market segment, or change the rules of the game. Examples? Sure ...

Examples of differentiated products and services are "everywhere." Like Rolls Royce automobiles, Nordstrom's personal shoppers, private banking, and generic drugs.

As for focusing on a specific market, Wal-Mart launched its business by opening its stores in smaller U.S. cities. The company thus gave small-town shoppers the opportunity to buy name brand merchandise at a discount.

Changing the rules of the game

Dell Computer changed the rules of the game. In the late 1980s, the manufacturers of personal computers felt relatively secure in their market share. In fact, IBM and Compaq "owned" the market for PCs. Then, in 1987, a young entrepreneur named Michael Dell decided he'd launch a company based on a new business model. Dell Computer entered the industry with a custom ordering system and a three-day, build-to-order process which eliminated inventory, and thus the costly depreciation on inventory. Dell charged their customer's credit card upon shipping the computer – just three days after receiving the order. And since Dell paid its suppliers in fifteen days, the company worked on a twelve day positive cash flow. Not bad! Young entrepreneur Michael Dell redefined how computers would be sold profitably. Much to the dismay of his competitors, he clearly changed the rules of the game.

Book seller Amazon.com also changed the rules of the game. The company launched its business using a spectacular web site. That web site offers as much – in fact, *more* – information about a book than you'll find in a book store. Certainly, Amazon.com offers a greater selection of books than you'll find in any store. Likely at a lower price, too. And shipped directly to your home or office.

Not necessarily high tech

But don't think that changing the rules of the game need be based on high tech. Here's a low-tech example from yesteryear ...When launching the first solid (plastic, rather than leather) ski boot way back in the 1960s, Rosemont Engineering Company changed the rules of the game. They raise-lettered the name "ROSEMONT," in big, bold letters across the bottom of the boot. But they *reversed* the letters – so the wearer of the boot imprinted "ROSEMONT" all over the snow. Imagine that – imprinting the company name all over the snow! Why, nobody had ever done that before! That's exactly the point. Rosemont changed the rules of the game.

Whether differentiating product or service, focusing on a specific market segment or changing the rules of the game, successful companies are *not* copying. They're innovating. Doing something different. Exercising entrepreneurial flair. And winning.

Diminishing Returns

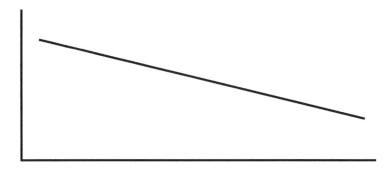

About three years ago, I worked with a client in the financial services industry. During one of the company's strategy sessions, the management team expressed frustration about what they called "deteriorating conditions in the marketplace." One of the managers exclaimed in frustration, "It used to be easier."

The scene wasn't at all unusual. This same frustration is shared by many others. In fact, this management team was simply experiencing "the law of diminishing returns." You do know about the law of diminishing returns, don't you?

In 1817, the British economist David Ricardo (1772-1823), developed what he then called, "the Law of Comparative Advantage." In developing that law, Ricardo dealt with the use of land. He observed that farmers, attempting to optimize their yields, cultivated their most productive land first. Only when the demand for farm commodities outstripped their production capabilities would farmers begin to cultivate less productive lands, such as rocky fields and steeper hillsides. Naturally, those less productive lands yielded diminishing returns on the farmers' added investment.

Ricardo's law applies to many other natural phenomena. Consider water wells, for example. Increased pumping due to expanding population or a hike in agricultural irrigation lowers the water table. This makes water more expensive to remove from the ground. And diminishes the return on investment in drilling and pumping.

Consider the California gold fields. In 1848, James Marshall discovered gold *lying on the ground* at Sutter's Mill. Those were the good old days! Over time, gold became harder and harder to find. Miners first combed the ground. Then panned the rivers. Then scratched the earth. Then picked their way into the earth. Then blasted. Then tunneled. Then spent millions and millions of dollars on modern mining equipment (also made from materials wrenched from the earth). Every step of the way – diminishing returns.

Ricardo's principle of diminishing returns applies in business as well. Managers encounter diminishing returns whenever they attempt to utilize "too much" of a single resource disproportionate to other resources.

Think about personnel. People represent the most obvious diminishing return. Sure, you can get more work out of your staff by asking them to work overtime. And you can do that a little bit. Enough to get 10%, or 15%, perhaps 20% more production. And you can do it for a while. A week or two. A month perhaps. But not much longer. People can't sprint forever. Diminishing returns.

Consider selling. You may begin with an excellent prospect list. Begin to sell to those prospects – in person, by phone or through the mail. Keep doing it. You'll note that, after some time, your returns will diminish. The "well is going dry" because you've already sold to most of the "real live" prospects on the list. You've picked up the nuggets lying on the ground. Now you've got to scratch away at the earth. Diminishing returns.

And think about production. Automating production is often an excellent strategy. Automation improves production rates, reducing costs per unit, thus making the company more competitive. Typically, it also increases product quality through improved process control.

But, too much automation leads to inflexibility in the organization. A product that must be manufactured "just like this" because "we've got a big investment in tooling." Or a product or service we're "stuck with" because we've got such a large investment in automated equipment that we can't afford to stop. Over-automation can lead to an organization setting strategy based on what piece of equipment happens to be sitting on the factory floor – rather than on what the customer wants to buy. Again, diminishing returns.

And consider finance. Adding debt to the company's capital structure may make lots of sense. Financial leverage can improve return on investment. To a point. Too much debt increases the level of debt service (payment on borrowed money) necessary, thus diminishing returns. Also, the added debt payment increases the firm's vulnerability to economic downturn.

Clearly, you've got to invest resources. And take risks. That's what business is all about. But keep Ricardo's principle in mind. And make sure your invested resources are in balance. That you're not investing in one resource disproportionate to the others. That you're not inviting a diminishing return on your investment.

Play the Game, Not the Shot

I went to college with a fellow named Tony DiNardo. Tony was an excellent pool player. And I don't just mean excellent, I mean EXCELLENT! Tony's dad ran the local distributorship for

Brunswick, the manufacturer of bowling, billiard, and pool equipment. So each day, after school, Tony went down to the Brunswick showroom "to help his dad in the business."

First, he did his homework, and then he'd shoot pool. All by himself, for a couple of hours each day, Tony would practice shooting pool. Seems he'd done this since the fifth grade. Oh, I'm sure that Tony had a natural talent for the game. That plus all the hours of practice, over all the years, made Tony a phenomenon at pool.

I played pool with Tony just once, and I hardly got in a shot. For he "ran the table" (sunk all 15 balls, in order, numbers 1 through 15) twice in a row! But while standing there in awe, I did learn a valuable lesson. For as he sunk ball after ball, Tony instructed me to "Play the game, not the shot." By that he meant, while shooting at any particular ball, be sure to leave the cue ball (the single white ball which the player hits into any other ball, with the intent of "sinking" that other ball into a pocket) in position for the next shot. Tony took his time between shots, thinking not so much about how to sink the ball at which he was then shooting. Rather, he focused on where he'd position the cue ball for the following shot.

Tony's lesson about "playing the game, not the shot," works in the world of business as well as in pool. For Tony's philosophy of the game is one of focusing on the longer, rather than the shorter term. When designing a new product, assure its quality and manufacturability, rather than focusing solely on completing its development. When selling a product or service, work on building a relationship with your customer, not so much the immediate sale. When hiring a new employee, consider not just what she'll work on the next morning, but also her capacity to grow with your organization.

Spectacular Customer Service

Less than a year after playing pool with Tony, I had a delightful experience with a company that clearly "focused on the game." In the summer of 1960, about to enter my sophomore year in engineering school, I had just purchased a slide rule. (Just in case you're too young to remember slide rules, they were the predecessors of hand held calculators.) Though I knew just enough to use its most basic scales, I was certainly eager to learn more, and to use my new slide rule during the coming school year.

Then the accident occurred. A couple of weeks before class began, I dropped the slide rule and shattered the cursor – that little glass window with the fine line scribed on it.

I was frantic! With the school year about to begin, I was without the ability to calculate. I was in big trouble. Doomed to failure, or so I feared.

In panic, I penned a letter. And I do mean *penned* a letter; for as a nineteen-year-old "kid," I didn't have access to a typewriter. (No personal computers in those days.) I penned a letter on a plain piece of paper to "Dear Sir or Madam at the Post Slide Rule Company."

In my letter, I wrote, "I'm nineteen years old, and I'm in big trouble! I dropped my slide rule, broke the glass cursor, and I need a replacement." And if Dear Sir or Madam would tell me where and how I might purchase a new cursor, I would be sure to hurry up and do so.

All this while, it hadn't even occurred to me that this incident wasn't going to mark the end of my career, I'd likely make it in life after all, and the school book store would gladly sell me a replacement cursor for thirty-five cents.

Exactly seven days after mailing my letter, I received a small package from the Post Slide Rule Company. The package contained a replacement cursor.

So here was this cursor – along with a letter from a fellow who happened to be the marketing manager of the Post Slide Rule Company. He, by the way, *did* have a typewriter. He said, in his letter, that he was sorry about the accident. "Here's a replacement cursor – with my compliments. Thank you very much for using our products, and best of luck in the coming school year."

The Post Slide Rule Company was in the business of selling *products*. But its marketing manager taught me that *providing service* is the key to keeping customers faithful. Faithful – oh yeah, I need to tell you one more thing …

About five years later, following graduation from engineering school, I was in a position to specify drafting supplies for the engineering firm for which I then worked. Can you guess what percentage of the drafting supplies I specified were those of the Post Slide Rule Company? Yep, you're right. Customer service pays. The Post Slide Rule Company benefited from "focusing on the game." Tony's lesson was correct.

(By the way, slide rules quickly became obsolete with the advent of hand-held calculators. In 1972, Hewlett Packard launched their HP 35 hand-held calculator. In just one year, from 1973 to 1974, the sales of slide rules dropped by 83 percent! An interesting case of technological product obsolescence.)

PART II

MARKETING

CHAPTER 5

THE
PRODUCT LIFE CYCLE

I'm sure that the Product Life Cycle is the most widely known of all business models. (See Figure 5 - 1.) Most business managers have run into the model at some point during their career. Or at least, they've learned about it in school, probably in their very first marketing class.

But, while most business managers have some familiarity with the model, few are familiar with its strategic implications. Let's take a look at the model, see just how it works, and discuss business strategies appropriate to each of its four phases.

The model shows industry-wide sales during the four phases of a product's "life cycle" along a time axis. Those phases are: Introduction, Growth, Maturity and Decline. We'll discuss each of those phases in just a moment, but first, I want to say a few words about the name of the model, for the name "product life cycle" is actually misleading.

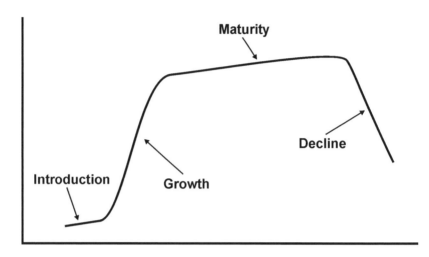

Figure 5 - 1: The Product / Service Life Cycle

It's misleading for two reasons. First, because it suggests that the model works for products but not necessarily for services. However, the model also works for services. It works just as well for cellular telephone service and ski instructions as it does for automobiles and wrist watches. Services experience the very same four distinct phases: introduction, growth, maturity and decline.

Second, the name is also mis-leading because it suggests that it's the *product* (or, as we've said, the service) that goes through four distinct phases. But during these four phases, the product or service doesn't necessarily change at all. Instead, it's the *market demand* that changes from one phase to the next. So as we look at the model, let's keep in mind that we're looking at a "picture" of changing market conditions. That is, we're watching the market demand for a product or service move through four distinct phases.

The Introduction Phase

Okay, with that note in mind, let's take a look at the Product Life Cycle. We'll begin with the first of the four phases, the Introduction phase. The first important question is: "What happens during the introduction phase?" Well, for one, we can see that industry-wide sales are low. That's no surprise, for the product or service has just been introduced. Not many people yet know about it, so sales are understandably low during this phase. The company offering the new product or service is busily promoting it so that folks will know it's available and, hopefully, understand that they need it. If that happens, sales will grow.

This combination of low sales and high promotional costs suggests that profits are negative during this first phase of the product life cycle. Indeed they are. It generally takes quite an investment to launch a new product or service both because of its initial development and also because of the need to promote it.

And consider this: during the introductory phase, every customer is a brand new customer. This means that the providers of new products and services must educate their potential customers as to the benefits of their offering. This is generally quite expensive. In the introduction phase, the name of the game is "pioneering." You'll need to pave new ground by teaching your customers about a product or service they've never heard of before.

If your company is the first to introduce a particular new product or service, you'll enjoy a specific advantage. During this phase, and *only* during this phase, you'll have the opportunity to be alone in the mind of your customer as the one and only supplier of this new product or service. You've pre-empted everybody else, and it's time for you to take advantage of this fact. When your customers, or your prospective customers, think of this new product or service, they've got to think of your company's name as well.

As Coke is to soft drinks, as Hertz is to auto rentals, and as IBM is to mainframe computers, you're out to establish – in the mind of your customer – your brand name in association with your product or service. You won't ever have this particular competitive advantage again (at least not with this product or service), so make the most of it.

The Growth Phase

Following successful promotion of the product or service, its demand moves from the introductory phase to the growth phase. Here, two things have changed. First, prospective customers have "caught on" to the benefits of using (thus purchasing) the product or service. Thus, sales volume has developed momentum. This momentum might be due to any combination of continued promotion, word of mouth recommendation, and repeat purchases.

The second factor that has changed is profitability. As those companies offering the product or service are now enjoying substantial sales, they are (perhaps at long last) covering their cost of promotion. And so, they're making a profit. This indeed is an exciting time for those offering the product or service. Rapidly growing demand combined with profitability. In fact, profitability is generally quite high. That's because supply is racing to catch up with demand. An entrepreneur's dream.

Attracted by the irresistible combination of rapid growth and profitability, a number of competitors will enter the marketplace. Naturally, they'll each fight for market share. You've got to do the same. Why? Because at the end of the growth phase, the industry will enter a shakeout. A shakeout that not all competitors will survive. You want to be sure that your company survives. So work to capture a significant market share. First place would be best. Second may be OK. Third or fourth place is dangerous.

The Shakeout

But why a shakeout? The shakeout occurs because of two coincident factors. First, customers will, sooner or later, figure out that they're already buying just about as much of the product or service as they actually need. Oh, sales will probably continue to grow, but at a significantly lower rate than during the growth phase.

The second factor causing the shakeout is the industry's overcapacity. Recall that, during the growth phase, competitors entered this lucrative market. And those competitors added more and more capacity, each attempting to grab additional market share. When market demand flattens (and sooner or later, it will), the situation becomes especially bad for those with significant unused capacity.

So watch for the end of the growth phase. Figure out "how much is enough." If you can accurately determine the eventual steady-state level of market demand – and thus accurately anticipate the coming of the shakeout – you'll avoid the terribly expensive problem of building capacity for forecasted sales growth that never happens.

To the best of your ability, go into the shakeout with a very significant market share (a leadership position would be wonderful!), with near-full, rather than excess capacity, and in a strong financial position.

The Maturity Phase

As the market moves beyond the shake-out, it enters the far more stable, and generally far longer-lasting, maturity phase. This maturity phase is stable because a limited number of competitors "share" the marketplace now characterized by slow growth. There isn't much investment in increased capacity because there isn't much growth in market demand to absorb that increased capacity. Generally, a fixed number of competitors serving a no growth, or a modest growth, market.

During this long, stable period of maturity, growing your sales will require that you "steal a customer from someone else." And you can do that in just two ways. You can either sell the same thing for less or you can sell something different (and presumably better). That means you'll need to be either the low-priced provider (based on your lower cost structure), or you'll need to differentiate. In fact, the maturity phase is generally characterized by competitive attempts to differentiate in one way or another. For example, Marriott Hotel, Marriott Courtyard, and Marriott Suites each target a different segment of the business travel market. Motel 6 claims that, "We'll leave the light on for you." They're attempting to suggest a point of differentiation in the hospitality industry. For the same reason, you can buy Lite beer, menthol tip cigarettes, and low-fat ice cream.

The Decline Phase

The decline phase follows maturity as products and services move toward obsolescence. The demand for some products – such as half-gallon containers of milk, and for some services, such as appendicitis operations – tend not to decline. Indeed, some products and services continue in the maturity phase seemingly forever. But most products and services do, sooner or later, experience a decline in market demand, thus a decline in sales.

During the market decline phase, you'll need to develop new products or services. Your strategy is replacement. From black-and-white television to color. From the Pentium 3 chip to the Pentium 4. From last year's model, to this year's. From milk in a bottle to milk in a wax paper carton. In all cases, something to invigorate sales, not of the declining product or service, but sales of your total line of products and services.

Conclusion? It isn't enough to understand the different phases of the product life cycle. If you're really going to bring benefit to your organization, you and your management team will also need to understand the appropriate strategies to use during each of the model's four phases.

A Successful Market Introduction

In the early 1970s, the Alpenlite Company executed an outstanding market introduction. The company was then a new start-up in the field of backpacking and mountaineering equipment. Its first product was an innovative backpack. In addition to its extremely large size, Alpenlite's backpack offered a number of other interesting features. For one, its solid external frame was designed so the backpack would stand up all by itself. Thus, the user could set it down on the ground and expect it to remain upright. He didn't have to lean it against a rock, a tree, or a fellow backpacker.

Alpenlite's backpack was also outstanding by its color. Until that time, backpacks were the traditional olive drab, dark green or Boy Scout Brown. But the big backpack from Alpenlite was bright orange.

Finally, the Alpenlite backpack was unique in its price. While other high quality backpacks then sold for $50 to $60 or so, the big orange giant was priced at *$100*.

Since nobody had ever heard of Alpenlite, the company's managers wondered, "How in the world are we going to compete for customer awareness against our already-established competitors?" Well, Alpenlite's managers solved that problem. Boy, did they! They came up with a very interesting – and very successful – marketing strategy. Alpenlite invested *one dollar!*

They went to the local backpack supply store and bought a copy of the *Sierra Club Schedule*. That schedule lists all the nifty backpack trips sponsored by the Sierra Club. In the back of the schedule, the Sierra Club lists the names and addresses of all the leaders of the Club's scheduled outings – about 800 leaders in the Southern California Chapter's schedule alone.

Next, Alpenlite wrote a letter to every one of the leaders listed in *The Sierra Club Schedule*. That letter said, "Dear leader; Here's the deal… We'd like your help in evaluating our new backpack. So, with your permission, we'll send you one of our new, super-large, very orange, stand-up-by-itself backpacks. It's yours to use for the entire summer season – no charge. At the end of the summer, you'll have two options:

- Option #1: You keep the pack and send us $50 – just half the retail price – along with your written evaluation of the pack.
- Option #2: You return the pack – again, no charge. You'll have had use of the backpack for the entire summer and, if you elect not to keep it, simply return it with your written evaluation. No cost to you."

I don't know how many backpacks Alpenlite sent out. Or the percentage of backpacks returned. That isn't what matters. What matters is that during that summer, a whole bunch of orange backpacks were walked about the mountains. Suddenly, a company whom nobody ever heard of got their product out there "in the field."

And who was wearing the orange backpacks? *The people at the front of the line*, that's who. The leaders! The people whom outings participants look to for guidance and advice. Alpenlite not only got out to the market, but they got to the most influential group of individuals in their marketplace. The *opinion setters*.

Result: Alpenlite went on the map overnight.

The B&B Food Market

Back when I was a small boy, my dad owned and operated a grocery store in New York City. Like most other independent grocers, he worked long and hard to eek out a modest living. Then, about 1950, supermarkets started becoming a major force in the grocery industry. And guess what? Just one block away from my dad's store, a new A&P supermarket opened for business. At the time, A&P was the dominant supermarket chain in New York – growing fast and driving out the independents one after another.

Sure enough, with the opening of the A&P just a block away, my dad's business suffered immediately. In fact, it initially looked as if he would have to close up shop.

However, at the same time that the supermarkets were expanding rapidly, an interesting demographic change was occurring in New York. Puerto Rican people were beginning to immigrate to New York City. And my dad's store was right in the middle of the neighborhood into which they were moving.

Dad recognized this as an opportunity. I'm sure he'd never heard the term "niche market," but that didn't slow him down at all. He found importers who'd supply tropical fruits and vegetables. He bought rice in hundred pound sacks. And he got Del Monte and Hunt's to deliver canned goods with Spanish language labels.

And it wasn't just the products. Seems like overnight, Dad learned to speak Spanish. The way I remember it, on Tuesday morning he couldn't speak a word, and by Friday evening he was fluent. Dad hired two helpers, Jerry and Charlie, both recent arrivals from Puerto Rico. And dad had all his signs – both inside the store and outside the store – printed in Spanish.

He changed the whole ambiance of the store. His customers, all recent immigrants from Puerto Rico, felt "right at home" (*en su casa*) shopping in his store.

As the neighborhood grew more and more ethnically Puerto Rican, my dad took lots of business away from the A&P supermarket.

CHAPTER 6

THE

OPPORTUNITY GRID

O f the various business models I use at strategy sessions, the Opportunity Grid is most popular among my clients. The model is actually a modification of Steiner's "Product and Market Matrix" (see George A. Steiner, *Strategic Planning: What Every Manager Must Know*, The Free Press, 1979).

George A. Steiner, Ph.D., Professor Emeritus at UCLA, originally developed his matrix specifically for products, but I realized that those of us in service industries could easily adapt it. Thus, while Steiner labeled the horizontal axis: "Products," I've labeled it: "Products or Services." About ten years ago, a client of mine began referring to the model as "The Opportunity Grid." The name stuck.

Here's how the model works. (See Figure 6 - 1.) We divide the horizontal axis, labeled Products / Services, into three categories – Current, Related, and Unrelated. So the three resultant columns represent *current* products or services, *related* products or services, and *unrelated* products or services.

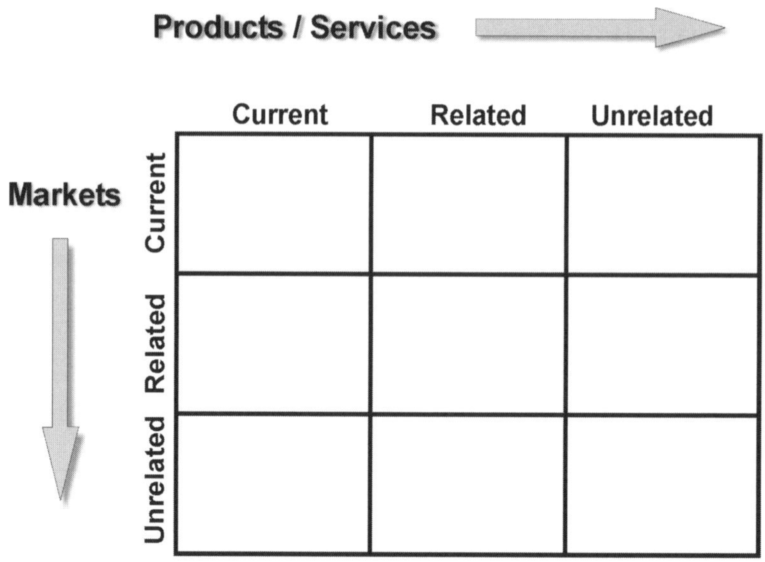

Products / Services

	Current	Related	Unrelated
Current			
Related			
Unrelated			

Markets

Figure 6 - 1: The Opportunity Grid

Similarly, we also divide the vertical axis, representing the markets for the company's Products / Services into the same three categories – Current, Related and Unrelated. Thus the three resultant rows represent *current* markets, *related* markets and *unrelated* markets.

Right now – today – every organization sells its current products or services to its current markets (or, in a narrower sense, to its current customers). This means that, in the present, every organization operates in the upper left box of the model. Only in the future could an organization venture out into the world of new product or service, or new markets. Thus, only in the future could a company expand beyond the model's upper, left box.

As strategy is about choice, every company's management team gets to decide whether to venture out along the path of product or service development (moving horizontally to the right in the model) or market development (moving vertically down in the model). Their choice would logically be based upon the company's preparedness for developing new products or services as compared to their preparedness for developing new markets. A management team's decision would thus be based on their company's internal strengths.

Were the management team to decide on product / service development, they'd next have to choose just how far to the right they'd move – either into the box representing related products or services, or into the box representing unrelated products or services. What differentiates related products or services from unrelated products and services? Great question! In fact, it is the exploration of that very question that results in the management team's deeper understanding of the organization and of its fundamental strengths and weaknesses.

As an example, a client of ours develops and markets software for the hospitality industry. When you walk into a hotel and step up to the front desk to check in, the desk clerk taps on a keyboard and stares into the computer screen searching for a record of your reservation. The software that the desk clerk thus uses is appropriately called "front office software."

OK, let's consider what might be a related product for this particular software developer. How about back office software? That's the software used by hotels to manage, not the guest's check in / check out, but rather the "business end" of the hotel's operation – staffing, accounts payable, cash flow, inventory levels, etc. The software developer's management team might well decide that any software related to the hospitality industry was a related product. Thus, everything else in the world – including software for any other application – would be an unrelated product. Why such a narrow definition? Because the company's managers have extensive experience in the hospitality industry. Any other application would thus be "foreign," or outside of the firm's core competency.

On the other hand, that same management team might instead decide that their critical skill is in software development, so they might decide that development of software for *any* application would constitute a related product.

Which decision is correct? The answer to that question would require a deep exploration of the company's core competencies based on the management team's deep understanding of their business. And this in-depth exploration – thus the management team's arrival at such in-depth understanding – is exactly what should happen at any strategy session. Hence the value of the Opportunity Grid in stimulating deep thought, deep discussion and deep understanding.

Just as the management team gets to decide whether to venture out into either related or unrelated product / service development, the team must also decide on the degree to which it might venture out into new markets. Either into related new markets or into unrelated new markets.

For example, let's consider the case of one of our clients, an insurance company specializing in providing insurance coverage for automobile rental agencies. The planning team might question whether providing insurance for automobile *sales* agencies is a related product. After all, it's one more market in the automobile industry. But upon further discussion, the planning team might conclude that a "related" market would instead be another rental operation. The team might conclude that the important factor in the related / unrelated decision is the *rental* aspect of the business rather than the *automotive* aspect of the business. Thus, rental of boats, airplanes and water skis would be related, while sales of automobiles would be unrelated.

How to Use the Opportunity Grid

During strategy sessions, we ask our clients to map their available opportunities on the Opportunity Grid. Some opportunities call for product or service development, but not market development, such as McDonalds expanding its menu to include salads in addition to hamburgers and fries. Clients map such opportunities in either the related product / service or the unrelated product / service box along the top row on the grid (see Figure 6 - 2).

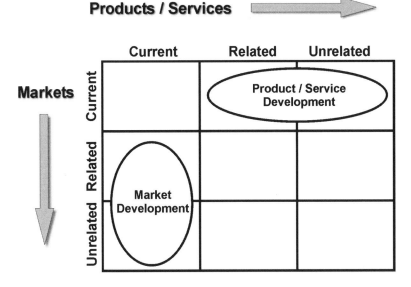

Figure 6 - 2: Mapping Opportunities

Other opportunities call for market development, but not product or service development, such as when Arm & Hammer began marketing its baking soda to deodorize refrigerators. Clients map these opportunities in either the related market box or the unrelated market box along the left hand column on the grid.

And then there are those opportunities that call for product / service development and also market development. Clients map these opportunities diagonally down and to the right of the current / current box. These opportunities require that the company utilize its know-how and expend resources in both product / service development and also in market development. Requiring "action" in both product / service development, and also in market development, the pursuit of such opportunities is more complex, thus more risky, as when Arm & Hammer brought out a toothpaste based on its baking soda product.

Not that the company shouldn't ever pursue such opportunities. At times, their pursuit might prove to be an excellent strategy. It's simply that the management team should be aware of the added complexity, thus the added risk of strategies calling for both product / service and also market development.

At times, though certainly not always, it's possible for a company to move in one direction at a time, thus accomplish a diagonal move in two steps. Using this two-step method, the firm can avoid the risk of simultaneous development in both product / service and also in marketing. As an example, let's return to the company currently offering insurance for auto rental agencies. Let's suppose that some of the company's auto rental agency customers also offer leases (as well as rentals) of automobiles. The insurance company might then develop a new policy specifically for automobile leases and offer that policy to its current rental / lease customers. The insurance company has thus moved to the right on the Opportunity Grid – selling a new product (probably a related product) to its current market – in fact, to a segment of its current customers.

After proving its new product in auto leasing, the insurance company might later – say in a year or two – offer the lease policy to boat leasing customers, or airplane leasing customers, or computer leasing customers. In each case, the insurance company would move vertically down into new markets (either related or unrelated).

Generally, it takes more time to develop new products and services, or to develop new markets, than to improve current operations. So strategies in other than the upper left box typically require more time to implement. And, if implementation time increases as you depart from the upper left box, what happens to risk? Generally, risk also increases. Typically, it is more risky to expand outside of the present business. That is, outside present products and services, and present markets. More risky because new products, services and markets involve development in relatively unfamiliar territory.

There are instances, however, when it is more risky to take the short-term approach – to stay with current products and services and current markets. It is more risky to do so when there is significant *change* in market demand. That change might be either growth in market demand, or decline in market demand. Regarding growth, information technology providers, for example, would be very foolish to attempt selling, in the long term, current products and services to current markets. Technological advances in their industry make it impossible for them to think in terms of doing the same thing – same products, same markets – three years from today, for example, that they do today. Their technology, and thus their customers' needs, are simply changing too quickly. In fact, over the last two decades, the power of personal computers has doubled every 18 months.

As for decline in market demand, consider a product or service nearing the end of its life cycle. Here, too, it's risky to attempt selling the same products and services to the same markets. The market in the United States for men's hats has been declining for some decades. The same is true for ladies' fur coats. Providers of such products should have been (certainly by now) broadening their offering to include products in earlier phases of their life cycle.

There isn't any one "right way" for a company to grow. No singular answer that says: "Develop products and services but not markets." No singular rule that states: "Don't dare move into unrelated markets." It depends on the firm's position in the marketplace, its internal strengths and weaknesses, and its external opportunities and threats. Here, like everyplace else, there's no substitute for knowledge, experience, and managerial judgment.

Perhaps you and your management team have a half dozen opportunities worthy of consideration. If so, map them on the Opportunity Grid. Talk about each during your next strategy session. You'll be pleased at the depth of your team's discussion. And the resulting deeper understanding of your enterprise.

CHAPTER 7

SELLING TO
YOUR PEERS

About five years ago, I worked with the research and development department of a major electronics company in California's Silicon Valley. Seems the organization was having a terrible time developing products that proved successful in the marketplace. One after another, the firm's new products missed their mark.

From the discussions at the company's strategy sessions, I learned that the R&D engineers were out of touch with the users of their products. So I asked the engineers, "How many visits to customers has each of you made during the last year?" The number of customer visits which each engineer reported ranged from zero to one. Zero to one! No wonder the company's new products missed their mark.

Clearly, the folks who were responsible for developing new products were out of touch with those who would purchase and use those products. Oh sure, the company did have a sales department. And those in the sales department did visit customers. But the sales force sold existing products and did not develop new products. However, the engineers did. Unfortunately, the sales force and the engineers didn't talk to each other about the wants and needs of their customers. Without ever intending to do so, the sales force acted as a buffer that kept the engineers away from customers. And, in the end, caused new products to miss their mark.

Pretty typical problem. Particularly with highly technical products. I've seen it in my own career. Ah yes, my own career …

I grew up in the world of electronics instrumentation, of engineers and high tech, of product development. And as my career advanced from the laboratory to the conference room, I noticed an interesting thing. Whenever a prospective customer is considering his first purchase of a particular technical product, both the person buying and the person selling must be educated in the technology of that product. The complexity of the product dictates that communication take place on a technical level – "engineer to engineer," as I call it.

The buyer needs to understand the product's specifications and features, and how to apply the product for his specific requirement. He needs to understand how to use the product; how to maintain, modify and repair it. And this information, in the detail required, can come only from a technical person on the selling side. A technical person who is truly a *peer* of the buyer.

Seems obvious, doesn't it? So how come the following scenario occurs far too often …

A technical products company hires a new salesman who has good selling skills but only limited technical knowledge. The company's advertising generates an attractive sales lead in the new salesman's territory. The new salesman goes out to call on the prospect.

The prospective customer expresses interest in the product but needs specific technical information beyond which the salesman is able to provide. According to the customer, there is "something different" about this particular application. (Ever heard that one before?)

The salesman sends four drawings and makes six phone calls, back to the factory, attempting to obtain information to satisfy the prospective customer's request for information.

Time goes by. The prospective customer begins to forget about the selling company, about the product, and also the name of the salesman. Suspecting he's beginning to lose favor with the prospective customer, the salesman grows more and more frustrated.

To stress the importance of the prospective account, the salesman places his seventh call to the factory "a level or two above proper channels." During his final call, the salesman may even be guilty of an exaggeration or two.

Finally, the salesman gets some support from the factory. An engineer from the factory boards an airplane to visit the prospective customer. During their meeting, the engineer and the prospect speak in the jargon of the industry and draw a diagram or two. The salesman looks on attempting, unsuccessfully, to understand the conversation.

The engineer flies home, and three days later sends the prospective customer a revised drawing and updated specifications. A week later, the engineer calls the prospective customer to again converse in technical jargon. Then – zippo! As if by magic, the salesman drives by the customer's office to pick up the purchase order.

And that's the way it works. It takes a selling technical person meeting with a buying technical person to consummate the buyer's first-time purchase of a technical product. And anyone else – a non-technical salesman on the seller's side or a purchasing agent on the buyer's side – will simply get pushed out of the way. *Every time.*

That doesn't mean you can't sell technical products using non-technical salesmen. You can. But you should recognize that, on the *initial* sale (and during much of the technical support which inevitably follows), the non-technical salesman is really a *finder.* He'll snoop out the prospect, get a rough idea of the potential order size and tell your engineer which airport to fly into. And if you expect much more, you'll waste a whole lot of money.

This engineer-to-engineer requirement is true in the various technical fields. I served on the board of two medical products manufacturing firms. In that industry, selling is best done by peers: by medical doctors or by scientists, able to look the doctor (customer) straight in the eye and explain, in technical terms, why this particular product is beneficial for that particular application. (By the way, I could also explain why it takes a management consultant to sell the services of a management consultant.)

In working with a number of Hewlett-Packard divisions, some years ago, I learned the term "next bench." A particular HP division designed and sold electronics laboratory equipment. Well, guess what? The HP design engineers were just like their customers. They used the very same equipment to perform very similar work. It was as if their customer were sitting at the "next bench." So HP's design engineers had an intimate understanding of their customers' needs.

Fish Talk

But the relationship between peers doesn't necessarily have to be technical. In fact, it can be just about any aspect of mutual interest. Quite a number of years ago, prior to launching my consulting practice, I worked for Microwave Instruments Company, a manufacturer of industrial moisture monitoring equipment. As the Technical Director for that firm, I traveled throughout the United States and Canada supporting our network of independent manufacturers' representatives. Specifically, I called on customers to help with the technical aspects of product applications.

On one occasion, Jimmy Bower, our sales representative in Louisiana, asked me to fly down to Baton Rouge to assist him in making a sale to a prospective customer. Jimmy figured that with technical back-up from the factory, he'd be able to close a deal for a moisture monitor at a large chemical plant. After discussing the situation with Jimmy, I booked my flight and was on my way.

The morning after my arrival, Jimmy picked me up at my hotel and we drove out to the customer's chemical plant. Arriving in the lobby, we told the receptionist that Mr. Clark was expecting us. Mr. Clark appeared in just a few minutes and the three of us were on our way to lunch. Mr. Clark sat in the front seat with Jimmy and I sat in back.

As we drove along a narrow country road through swamp country, Mr. Clark and Jimmy started with small talk. They talked about fishing. Seems that both were very much into fishing, which made sense to me as I'd heard that lots of guys in Louisiana liked to fish.

The restaurant was farther away than I had expected. It took us at least a half hour to get there. Both of the guys assured me that lunch would be well worth the wait. After all, we were going to a "joint" which served the best catfish in the county. After offering this assurance, the guys returned to talk about fishing.

I learned quite a bit during that forty-minute drive. I learned about which fishing holes were best for bass and which for catfish. And that catfish bite more aggressively when the sky is cloudy. Opinions seemed to differ, however, about which bait is best, particularly early in the season.

Upon arriving at the restaurant (yes, it was a joint), a tall, red-headed waitress named Lucy soon appeared at our table. She announced that the special for the day was catfish with jambalaya. Naturally, all three of us jumped at this opportunity.

While waiting for our food to arrive, the guys returned to their talk about fishing. Just once, Mr. Clark interrupted his fish talk to ask me a question about the response time of our moisture monitor. I answered his question, which I interpreted as his signal that the fish talk was now over – so we'd begin to "talk business." I asked Mr. Clark a question about his intended application of the moisture monitor. He replied with a much abbreviated description of his manufacturing process, remembered another fishing story he'd earlier forgotten, and turned toward Jimmy to relate that story.

Throughout the rest of that meal, and throughout our drive back to the chemical plant, the conversation stayed firmly anchored in fish talk. When we arrived back at his plant, Mr. Clark stepped out of the car and turned to thank us both for lunch. Then he added, "Say, you know that moisture monitor we've been talking about? Well, I think we'll actually need two rather than one. I'll have a purchase order for you tomorrow."

And so we had made the sale. Or at least Jimmy had made the sale. I hadn't done anything except pay for lunch. When I told Jimmy that he'd made the sale all by himself, he explained that I, too, had played an important role. He said that Mr. Clark had earlier been concerned about product support. He'd wondered if an equipment manufacturer way out west in California would be responsive to his needs. According to Jimmy, I did my part by flying across the country and showing up for lunch.

Hmmm… while that particular sale clearly wasn't one of my proudest accomplishments, I was certainly happy to receive the order for two moisture monitors. More importantly though, I learned an important lesson about selling to peers. The buyer-seller relationship doesn't necessarily have to be technical. It can also be based on a mutual interest … like fishing.

CHAPTER 8

SELLING STAPLES

I went to college with a fellow named Al Marko. One day, Al and I were talking about what we wanted to do when we graduated. Al said, "I want to own and operate a manufacturing business."

I asked the obvious question, "What do you want to manufacture?"

"Oh, some small parts," Al replied.

"What do you mean, 'Some small parts'? What kind of parts?"

"Oh, I don't care, just something small."

To my continued questioning, Al finally explained that the price of a small part generally goes unnoticed. So, the manufacturer could charge darn near anything he wanted.

To prove his point, he posed a compelling example. "Suppose a business executive were to write a four-page report. Likely the value of that report could be measured in hundreds, perhaps thousands, of dollars. Clearly that business executive never gives a moment's thought to the price of the staple in the upper left corner of his report." Al went on to explain that the same was true for paper clips, nuts and bolts, and coat hangers.

Seems that Al had made a good point.

I benefited from that conversation with Al. Many years later, while in the process instrumentation business, I successfully marketed temperature monitoring equipment by showing that a $5,000 investment would return $20,000 in energy savings, or $30,000 in increased product throughput. I actually thought of our monitoring equipment as a "small part." And, I referred to my marketing approach as "selling staples."

But, there are two serious limitations to Al's theory. First, the executive who develops the report may not be the same person who buys the staple. Especially in larger firms, the task of purchasing office supplies is generally left to a junior buyer. And, junior buyers really do care about the price of staples.

Clearly, this limitation is more serious in larger organizations where there's a greater distance from executive to junior buyer. We'd expect, therefore, that Al's theory would work better in smaller companies.

Well, it does work better in smaller companies. But we still need to talk about limitation number two, or what I call: "calibration of the mind." Just as our eyes are capable of adjusting to wide variations in the intensity of light, our minds are capable of adjusting (and calibrating) to wide variations in purchasing decisions. Yes, I'll explain …

Obviously, during the time the business executive is thinking about his $1,000 report, he's not going to consider the price of the staple. But later he might. Imagine this. One morning, you're in your office negotiating the purchase of a new computer system. Clearly, you're dealing with a decision involving thousands of dollars.

An hour later, you're looking over the lunch menu at a nearby restaurant. Certainly, your lunchtime decision involves far less financial risk. $6.75, $8.50, $17.50. Still, you consider, "I don't really want to spend that much money for lunch." See, you've re-calibrated your mind to the task at hand.

I envision a large man in a red cashmere sweater dining in a Las Vegas restaurant. He puts down his steak knife, slowly sips his $60 a bottle Cabernet Sauvignon, and complains to his dinner companions about the price of the morning newspaper.

I wonder what Al Marko is doing today.

Don't Fake It!

About three years ago, I worked with a mid-sized financial services firm. During our very first strategy session, three of the company's salesmen were talking about the various ways they might respond to a customer's question for which they didn't have an answer.

I offered my (strong) opinion that, "You should tell the customer that you don't know the answer, but you'll be happy to find out." I explained that, "You really can't fool the customer, so don't even try."

As the salesmen seemed unconvinced by my advice, I told them the following story ...

For quite a number of years now, I've enjoyed photography. Generally, I use black-and-white film and, often, I photograph landscapes. It's no surprise then, that I much admire the work of renown landscape photographer Ansel Adams. Adams was born in 1902 and passed away in 1984. Appropriately, the Ansel Adams Museum is in San Francisco, the city in which he grew up.

As I frequently travel to San Francisco for business, I often visit the Ansel Adams Museum. On one particular occasion, about eight years ago, I checked into the San Francisco Marriott and, as is my custom, I walked up to the concierge desk to ask about that week's exhibits in the Ansel Adams Museum. As I approached the concierge desk, I noted a new face. Though I'd stayed in the Marriott many times, I hadn't before seen this particular young lady. I figured she was new.

I asked her, "Could you tell me please, what's on display at the Ansel Adams Museum?"

She replied, "He's not always there."

Not wishing to be impolite, I didn't tell her that, were she referring to Ansel Adams, he'd been dead for well over a decade. I simply repeated her statement as a question, "He's not always there?"

"No, he travels a lot," she replied.

"Oh, he travels a lot?" I repeated, feigning surprise.

By now, she and I had established a sort of a rhythm to our conversation. Clearly, I was the straight man. "Yes, he travels a lot. And when he does, he takes much of his work with him."

I found that last comment particularly interesting. For me, it conjured up a vision of a dead photographer, standing behind a large view camera mounted on a sturdy wooden tripod – all the while holding a dozen or so framed photographs under each arm.

Before I could reply, "Oh, he takes much of his work with him, does he?" she added, "But the museum often displays the work of other photographers."

Ah, finally! Now I might actually get some useful (and true) information! I asked her, "Do you know which other photographers have their work on display at the museum this week?"

She reached for a copy of *What's Happening in San Francisco*, and began thumbing through the pages. Within a minute or so, I had my answer. I thanked her, and departed.

Two evenings later, I visited the Ansel Adams Museum. And, as it turned out, the young concierge was correct in that some other photographers had their work on display. I looked around for him, but Ansel Adams wasn't there that evening. He must have been traveling. And only a very few of his photographs were there on display. I suppose he took much of his work with him.

Moral of the story: Don't fake it. If you don't know the answer, say so. You really can't fool your customer. So don't even try.

PART III

PEOPLE

CHAPTER 9

DO YOUR EMPLOYEES REALLY CARE?

Developing your strategy is just the first big step. The second, and generally much larger, step is *implementing* your strategy. Implementing strategy is difficult because it requires change. In fact, you wouldn't even develop a strategy if you didn't want to bring about change … and presumably, change for the better.

But, for a variety of reasons, many employees feel threatened by change. Having a well-established power base, those in senior positions may perceive a redistribution of their authority. Others may feel threatened by the measurement system that necessarily accompanies strategy implementation. And at the very least, all are apprehensive about a disruption of the routine.

Apprehensive or not, individuals respond to change in different ways. Some welcome it; others don't. Their degree of acceptance or rejection depends on a number of factors: differing perspectives based on position within the organization, varying levels of risk tolerance, educational and intellectual preparedness, and inclination to focus on short-term versus long-term objectives.

Those who resist the implementation of strategy do so for one of three fundamental reasons. Some fear their inability to successfully implement the strategy. In dealing with such fear, your challenge will be to increase the employee's self-confidence. You'll need to provide the necessary training to improve employee skills, and offer encouragement through on-going communication. And, of course, you'll need to allocate resources sufficient to support the strategy's implementation.

A second reason why an employee might resist implementation is fear that the strategy simply won't work. That is, even though successfully implemented, the strategy won't achieve its intended objective. To counter an employee's concern (whether spoken or unspoken) that the strategy won't work, you'll need to *communicate*. Work toward mutual understanding by "selling" the employee on a broader point of view. And persuade as necessary. Hopefully, gentle persuasion will do the job. If not, then as a last resort, you'll need to persuade more strongly.

Finally, an employee may fear that, once implemented, the strategy will work *against* his own personal interests. To address such concerns, you'll have to deal with the employee's attitude and values. Again, you'll need to persuade – to show the employee that his individual payoff is actually more beneficial than he earlier thought. And if that payoff isn't actually greater, you might consider changing the reward system.

Regarding the reward system, some companies link financial compensation to strategy implementation. And that seems to make sense. After all, what better way to align your organization's objectives with those of the individuals who must accomplish them?

Caution however: Compensation systems require careful consideration. There can be problems, as when a strategy based on a planning team's faulty assumption can't be implemented – and the one individual assigned responsibility suffers financially. Or when a strategy has grown obsolete but those to be compensated for its successful implementation continue to "push."

Be especially careful that your reward system doesn't work to your company's disadvantage. A mid-sized, California manufacturing company had an unfortunate accident about ten years ago. During a late-night rain storm, water accumulated on the roof of the company's factory, and the roof collapsed. Not only did the roof collapse, but a large air conditioning unit fell through the roof onto the factory floor. Repair and replacement costs totaled $400,000. Fortunately, the incident occurred during the middle of the night when no one was in the factory.

You might ask, "How in the world could such a thing happen? Why did the roof collapse?"

The answer is "deferred maintenance." The roof was left to deteriorate for quite a number of years until, in its weakened condition, it couldn't support the water accumulating during the storm.

How come the roof was left to deteriorate? Why was maintenance deferred? Because were the roof to be maintained, then the maintenance expense would have been deducted from operating profit for the year. And the factory manager's bonus would have been reduced. Clearly, the company's reward system worked to its disadvantage.

One more point about financial rewards: While generally an effective motivating factor, they aren't necessarily "the whole story." Some employees desire more than the traditional extrinsic rewards (pay, promotion, security). Many individuals, particularly the more highly educated, also seek intrinsic rewards (self-satisfaction). In linking financial compensation to implementation, judgment is crucial.

Communicate

Whatever the form of resistance to strategy implementation, you'll benefit from applying a heavy dose of communication. But while it's easy to say you've got to communicate, you might ask, "Communicate how? Communicate when?"

First, it's important to note that communication works both ways. Both telling (speaking or writing) and also listening. Too many managers forget about the listening part. Listening is your key to understanding your employees' feelings about your strategy. About their level of enthusiasm for its implementation. About their specific fears. And just maybe – maybe your employees can offer an important insight about your strategy. You'll gain that insight only if you listen.

In the mid-1980s, a major beverage company developed a plan to construct a bottling plant in Central California. In developing that plan, top management worked directly with the architectural and contracting firms. But management never thought about discussing the project with mid and lower-level employees – the folks who operate the bottling machines, who stack the product for shipping, who drive the delivery trucks.

Upon completion of construction, hundreds of employees showed up for work. And guess what? The truck drivers took one look at the loading area and reported that they couldn't back their trucks up to the loading dock. It seems that the distance between the building and a block wall along the driveway was too small to allow for the wide turns necessary to back in a semi-truck. The truck drivers recognized this problem immediately. Too bad that management never thought to ask them about their space requirements.

Yes, the bottling plant finally did open … but only after some months, and some additional hundreds of thousands of dollars spent on plans, permits and re-construction – all unnecessary expenditures, easily avoided if management had only communicated, had only listened, to the folks who knew all along.

Remember, too, that communication is an on-going process. Not just a single memo or a brief meeting to announce a strategy, but an on-going process beginning early, well before strategy development, and continuing throughout the strategy's implementation.

As for the specific form of communication – one-on-one meetings, discussion group sessions or written documents – it depends on the specific situation. While it's impossible to make universal recommendations regarding which method of communication to use, here are some general guidelines:

- One-on-one meetings are useful for focusing on specifics – a specific individual's commitment, his perceptions, his fears, the tasks he is to perform.
- Group meetings are helpful for gathering input, for brainstorming ideas, and for building consensus.
- Written documents make official announcements, such as presenting a final strategic plan, a completed budget, or a project schedule.

Find the "Sweet Spot"

At an American Management Association Strategy Implementation Course, a participant asked me an interesting question. It seems that her planning team had devised a strategy, but her managers were struggling with its implementation. Upon further discussion, we (she, the other course participants and I) discovered that her employees lacked the necessary skills to fully implement the strategy.

As a tool in our understanding the problem, I drew two intersecting curves on the board. The first of those curves represents payback versus "stretch" (effort) required to implement a particular strategy. Conceptually, the greater the required stretch, the greater return you'd expect from having successfully implemented the strategy. Thus, this first curve slopes upward to the right. (See Figure 9 - 1.)

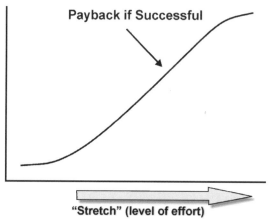

"Stretch" (level of effort)

Figure 9 - 1: Payback vs. "Stretch"

The second curve represents the probability of success for your strategy as a function of stretch. The more you ask your people to stretch, the more difficult will be the strategy's implementation. Thus, the lower will be its probability of success. So this curve slopes downward to the right.

Somewhere around the middle of the graph – in the neighborhood where the two curves intersect – is your "sweet spot." (See Figure 9 - 2.) That spot represents the appropriate level of stretch such that your return on the successfully implemented strategy is reasonably high. And so is your probability of successful implementation.

But, as a leader, it's your responsibility to increase the skills of your employees. Thus you'll be forever working at moving to the right on the second curve. (See Figure 9 - 3.) And, over time, you'll increase your probability of success with strategies calling for higher and higher levels of "stretch."

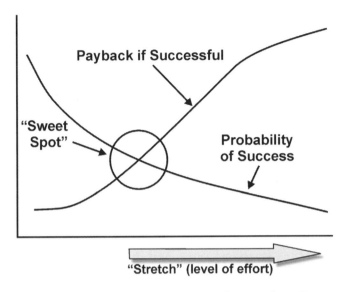

Figure 9 - 2: Finding the "Sweet Spot"

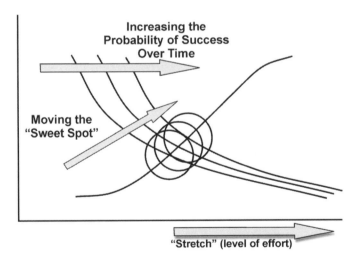

Figure 9 - 3: Moving the "Sweet Spot"

Options for Change

At times, to implement your strategy you'll have to increase the skill level of your employees. What options do you have for such change?

Actually, you have three options. First, you can simply wait for your employees to grow through experience. This choice offers the advantages inherent in evolutionary change. It's non-threatening and supportive of the existing culture. The disadvantage, of course, is that such evolutionary change is very slow. Thus it's generally not appropriate for a "revolutionary" strategy such as shifting from low to high technology, from industrial to consumer marketing, or from internal growth to growth through acquisition.

A second method for increasing employee skill level is to retrain. Faster, yes, but more costly. And it's also important to consider "what's realistic?" That is, whom can you retrain to do what? And how quickly? Training production workers to program automated assembly equipment is one thing; training them to *design* such equipment is quite another.

Finally, you can increase your employee skill level by hiring new people. While hiring can bring on change much faster, you'll run the risk of disrupting your company's existing culture.

Be careful to keep your expectations realistic; too many managers hope to solve all their problems by hiring "the great white knight." Hopefully, you don't really believe that the new marketing manager, yet to be hired, will research the market, specify the new product line, train the sales staff, decide on an appropriate level of market diversity, and solve the customer service problem … all within fourteen months. Be careful. Be realistic.

Winning an Argument

At an American Management Association Strategic Planning Course some years ago, the president of a mid-sized company shared an interesting story. He told of his organization's first experience with strategic planning. It seems that, on the third day of their three-day strategy session, his planning team considered two potential marketing strategies. One, which we'll call strategy "A," the president alone favored. All the other planning team members favored strategy "B."

After deliberating on the issue for 45 minutes or so, the team seemed stuck. The president realized he had a choice. He could have said, autocratically, "We've talked about this subject long enough. We're wasting valuable time. We're going to adopt my strategy – strategy A." His second choice was to yield and say, "Sure, I'm the boss, but I respect your overwhelming confidence in strategy B. Let's go with the consensus."

The president took this second choice. He agreed to strategy B. He did so because he felt the company would be better off with even a second-best strategy that the management team believed in rather than a first-best strategy that only he wanted. He was confident that after "selling" the boss on their strategy, his management team would be so totally committed that they'd do everything humanly possible to make their strategy work and prove themselves right to their president.

I'm not suggesting that such a decision is always correct. I'm not even certain that it was correct in this instance. I simply cite the case of a president who recognized the importance of managerial commitment to successful strategy implementation.

CHAPTER 10

HUNTERS, FARMERS, SHEPHERDS

My friend and former client, Bob Stollar, taught me the Hunters, Farmers and Shepherds model. According to that model, a business manager can be categorized as either a "hunter," a "farmer" or a "shepherd."

Hunters love to go out and "get the business." They're the sellers, the deal-makers. They're content to land the order, drive back to the office and toss the order onto somebody else's desk. They're perfectly willing to leave the building of the product, the providing of the service, the satisfaction of customer needs, to somebody else.

That "somebody else" is the Farmer. Farmers nurture the "crops" – the company's products and services. Farmers are concerned with quality, with details, with projects and processes. And they're often frustrated by Hunters' lack of attention to detail, lack of commitment to the product, and unwillingness to stick around longer than necessary to toss the order onto somebody else's desk.

Finally, Shepherds are the "people persons." For them, business is as much a social experience as it is an enterprise. Shepherds are easy to recognize. They're the folks who talk about employee training and development. And they spend lots of time inviting people to meetings. Shepherds are frustrated by Farmers' nose-to-the-grindstone attitude and the Hunters' maverick approach. Shepherds feel that Hunters and Farmers are missing an important dimension – the people dimension – in their work experience.

No manager fits perfectly into any of these three categories. There's some of the Hunter, the Farmer and the Shepherd in all of us. But each individual possesses a unique blend of the three. Within a triangle whose corners represent the three ways of thinking, each individual corresponds to a particular point, generally closer to one corner than the other two.

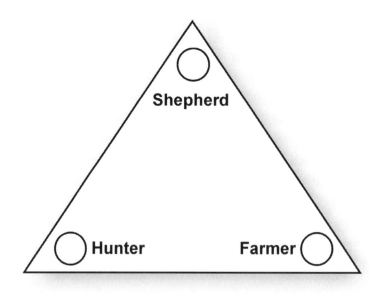

Figure 10 - 1: Hunters, Farmers, Shepherds

And think about this – every company needs a blend of all three activities: landing the order, providing the product or service, and maintaining the people relationships. All are necessary ingredients to organizational success. All three should contribute to the culture of the enterprise.

About ten years ago, I worked with a client company – a regional office of a large accounting firm. Almost immediately, I recognized that the partner managing a particular forty-person department was "all Hunter." In the parlance of the profession, he focused heavily on "practice development," i.e., on landing new clients.

And for the most part, his being a Hunter was fine. In the highly competitive public accounting industry, obtaining new clients had, by the early 1990s, become "the name of the game."

But his being a Hunter wasn't all good. In particular, it wasn't good for the staff reporting to him. His employees, each and every one of them, needed help. Needed help in the technical aspects of accounting, in their client relations, and in their own career development. Such help could come only from a partner who had time for them. From a partner who cared. From a partner who was, at least in part, Shepherd. To say the least, the department's staff was frustrated.

Fortunately, the senior partner in charge of the regional office was aware of the problem. He assigned another partner to "help manage" the department – and that partner was largely a Shepherd. This solution worked … sort of. The newly arrived "Shepherd" partner served to remind the "Hunter" partner of the needs of the department's managers. And the managers' needs were addressed … somewhat. And the effectiveness of the department improved … somewhat. But not as much as it would have improved if the partner managing the department had been more of a Shepherd.

Another client, a consulting firm headquartered in Southern California, opened an office in Denver to service the firm's largest on-going consulting assignment. The president of the firm, back in Southern California, looked to the Denver office for business expansion, for obtaining new accounts, and for growing into a "Rocky Mountain Regional Office."

But, after a whole year, the Denver office failed to obtain even a single new client and remained a project office, serving only the one large initial account. How come?

The reason was that the manager of the Denver office was a Farmer. Her skill lay in her ability to manage an already-contracted-for assignment. At that, she was superb. But the thought of practice development, of going out to obtain new business, scared her. Clearly, she wasn't a Hunter. But a Hunter was exactly what the Denver office needed to expand in the Rocky Mountain Region.

Actually, the firm did expand in the Rocky Mountain Region, but it wasn't easy. The Hunters based at Southern California headquarters, including the president himself, spent much time in Colorado drumming up business and getting the expansion off the ground. That expansion would have come far more easily if the Denver office manager were more of a Hunter.

While all three – Hunter, Farmer and Shepherd – are necessary ingredients, be careful. It's tempting to conclude that, ideally, the culture of the organization should be smack dab in the middle of the triangle. That is, to assume its culture must contain equal portions of Hunter, Farmer and Shepherd attitudes. But that isn't necessarily so.

Like everything else in life, it all depends. The "correct" culture for a particular company depends on its industry. Direct mail and door-to-door sales organizations, for example, focus most of their resources on selling. They're "correct" in adopting the attitude of the Hunter. The name of the game in their business is getting the order. Get the order, toss it on somebody else's desk, and go on to land the next order.

Companies in emerging industries tend to be product-driven, particularly during the early stages of their development. They're "correct" in thinking like the Farmer: develop a better mousetrap; invent something new; create a new product, a new service, or a new distribution system.

And many service organizations – particularly those in the helping professions such as health care, human services and education – are "correct" in adopting the emphasis of the Shepherd. These organizations deal in a service having a high human factors content. Theirs is a culture of people-orientation.

Also, small start-ups, focused on building the business, apparently adopt the emphases of the Farmer and of the Hunter. Later, with growth and with many more employees, they require the emphasis of the Shepherd.

Think about the managerial needs of your own organization. And about the tendencies of your managers. Call a meeting to talk about those needs ... *and* put some dots on the triangle. The Shepherds will love you for it.

But, for the sake of the Hunters, make the meeting short. They'll be eager to get back out in the field – so they can chase down the next order.

Value/Philosophy Choices

Quite a number of years ago, I developed the Value/Philosophy Choices Survey to:

- Encourage management team members to think strategically about their enterprise, and
- Uncover important issues that the management team needs to address during their up-coming strategy sessions.

The survey consists of eighteen sets of contrasting values or philosophies, arranged at opposite ends of a double arrow, as in Figure 10-2.

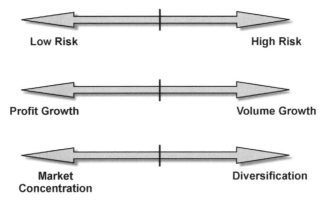

Figure 10 - 2: Value / Philosophies Choices

Here's how to use the survey:

1. First, ask each member of your management team to place an "X" on each line where his or her own value lies. That is, where he or she would *prefer* your organization operate.

2. Next, ask each person to place an "O" on each line indicating where they believe your organization *actually* operates. So when an individual is all finished with the survey, each line will have an "X" and an "O" on it – somewhere. The "X" indicates an individual's preference; the "O," his perception of reality.

3. Next ask each member of your management team to send their completed survey (or a copy of it) *anonymously* to whomever will compile all of the completed survey forms. The person who compiles the survey will begin with an identical blank survey form and copy all of the "X's" and "O's" onto that new form. The resultant compilation should offer some interesting revelations.

You might discover that your managers are split on whether they'd prefer a centralized or a decentralized organization (see Figure 10 - 3).

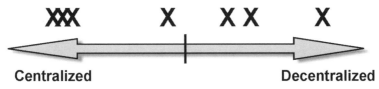

Centralized   **Decentralized**

Figure 10 - 3: Lack of Consensus Regarding Preference

Or you might discover that your team agrees that market diversity is desirable but perceives that your organization's market is currently concentrated rather than diverse (see Figure 10 - 4).

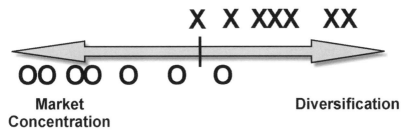

Market   **Diversification**
Concentration

Figure 10 - 4: Preference Differs from Perception

Or you might discover that your team members concur on the desirability of participatory management but are split on whether management is actually participative or authoritative (see Figure 10 - 5).

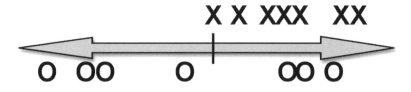

Authoritative   **Participative**

Figure 10 - 5: Lack of Consensus Regarding Perception

After compiling the surveys, make copies of the compilation for all of the planning team members. Then, at the opening of your strategy sessions, begin with a presentation of these findings. Your team will benefit from this information. You'll find it especially helpful in shedding light on your company's internal weaknesses.

We find that managers eagerly participate in the Value / Philosophies Survey and look forward to seeing the compiled results.

Here's a list of the 18 contrasting values / philosophies:

- Low Risk – High Risk
- Profit – Growth
- Controlled Growth – Aggressive Growth
- Return on Investment – Return on Sales
- Market Concentration – Diversification
- Austere Spending – Free Spending
- Authoritative – Participative
- Closed Information – Open Information
- Low Profile – Public Exposure
- Low Price Image – High Price Image
- Centralized – Decentralized
- Regional Markets – National Markets
- National Markets – International Markets
- Dividends – Retained Earnings
- Promote from Within – New Blood
- Management Interests – Stockholder Interests
- Product Follower – Product Innovator
- Formal Environment – Informal Environment

CHAPTER 11

MANAGING BY NEGLECT

Some years ago, I shopped frequently in a local map store, where I bought topographic maps for backpack trips to the mountains and deserts of the Western United States. A tall, dark-haired lady, about forty years old, worked in the store. Funny thing about that gal was that every time I visited the store, she was chewing gum … though presumably a different piece of gum each time.

And she collected cactus plants. All around the store, on shelves high and low, were potted cacti of many varieties. And those cacti – without exception – were beautiful specimens. The remarkable health of each and every plant surprised me, because cacti generally do far better raised outdoors.

One day, I mentioned to her that I'd been admiring her cacti and commented that they were in excellent health. "What do you fed them that they do so well?" I asked.

"Neglect," she replied.

Some things, it seems, are better off left to fend for themselves. Like cacti. Sure, they need soil. And light. And even some water now and again. But I know from experience, for I, too, collect cacti, that you can kill them with too much water, or even a small amount of fertilizer, or eleven other varieties of well-intended care.

Same with people. Oh not all people. Just a few. There are those few exceptional people who thrive not on close supervision – for that inhibits them – but on neglect.

Oh, not absolute neglect. Even the special few need fundamental support such as tools to work with, a comfortable environment, and occasional recognition. But they need – in fact, they thrive on – far less "attention" than most managers are comfortable providing. So they're best handled by managers willing to stand back, managing by a rather simple system of informal reporting.

But what makes for "cactus" type employees, those who thrive on neglect rather than close supervision? Two factors:

1. The employee must possess the fundamental skills to do his or her job, including both knowledge and experience.
2. The employee must also possess initiative, the drive that so often makes the difference between someone who simply does the job and the person who "shines."

First Rate People

Way back in 1977, Robert Stermer, then an executive with the Rockwell Corporation, said, "First-rate people hire first-rate people. Second-rate people hire third-rate people."

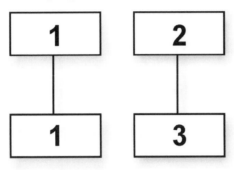

Figure 11 - 2:
First-Rate People Hire First-Rate People

Bob's right.

Think about it. Haven't you noticed a high correlation between top-performing executives and the top-performing people they hire? Haven't you observed that well-run, successful companies are led by first-rate executives? Executives who employ teams of first-rate people?

To first-rate people, the benefit of hiring other first-rate people is obvious. As workers, they don't have to be pushed. Managers simply need supply them with the tools to do their jobs, and stand back. Give them enough room, and they're motivated by their own commitment to perform.

As managers, first-rate people have strategic vision. They see the "big picture." They understand the company's objectives and embrace the fundamental strategies necessary to achieve those objectives. And their vision and understanding drives them toward growth.

And yet second-rate people hire third-rate people. They do so for any one of four fundamental reasons:

1. Second-rate people lack the judgment necessary to identify third-rate people as such. Since they themselves are second-rate, they're less sensitive to the deficiencies of others.

2. Second-rate people underestimate the importance of hiring first-rate people. Rather, they think in terms of "saving a few bucks" in salary. Penny wise.

3. Second-rate people are afraid of being challenged or rivaled by someone they hire, someone better than they are, and someone who may eventually get their job.

4. The best people – the first-rate people – turn down offers to work for second-rate bosses. They look instead for opportunities to work for first-rate bosses, for opportunities to grow.

Here's your choice. You can hire first-rate people and surround yourself with first-rate attitudes, with vision, with understanding, with enthusiasm, and with achievement.

Or you can hire third-rate people, put in your eight hours each day and look forward to retirement.

The Organization Chart

Conventional organization charts offer people outside the company a feel for who does what. But for those within the firm, organization charts can be stifling. They put people into neat little boxes, show who's "higher up" than whom, and suggest that relationships are based on a network of solid and dotted lines. They demonstrate where the official *power* is in the company.

But power doesn't count.

Here in the 21st century, employees expect a more participatory role in their working lives. They want choices. They want to be treated as partners in the decision-making process, and not as underlings. Today's workers are more informed, more intelligent and more individualistic. Knowledge workers, who "carry the business in their head," aren't powered into action. They're led.

And the picture of leadership isn't drawn with "the boss" at the top of the organization chart. The picture of leadership is one of support. So you'll benefit from an unconventional organization chart – one based on support.

That chart is an inverted pyramid with the boss at the bottom. Extending upward from the boss, are outstretched arms with hands supporting managers a level above.

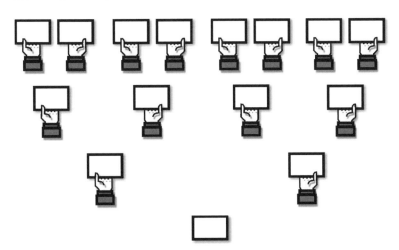

Figure 11 - 3: The Organization Chart

The chart continues in this inverted fashion with each succeeding level of managers supporting the next. Until, just below the very top, are those people "highest up" in the organization, those who actually make the product or deliver the service, those who actually do the work, those whose hands support the most important folks of all … the customers.

You can add names and titles to the chart if you wish, but I wouldn't. I think the chart itself tells the story.

And you know what? Through supporting employees, through leading them rather than powering them, through allowing them to participate in decisions that affect their jobs, you'll build their commitment. And there's nothing in the world like commitment for achieving a fun-to-work-in environment and a profitable, growing company at the same time.

What Is Delegation Anyway?

We often hear the criticism, "My manager seems unable to delegate." But what does this mean? What, specifically, do we mean by "delegation"?

First, delegation means *trust*. To delegate successfully, a manager must trust that employees can successfully handle the assignment, that they have both the skills and the resources to get the job done. And trust that, should they run into difficulty, they will appropriately ask for help.

It's also important to understand what you should, and should not, delegate. In short, effective delegation involves the manager telling the employee *what* to accomplish, and allowing the employee to figure out *how* to accomplish it. The "what to accomplish" is the employee's objective. The "how," which the employee then develops, is the method by which he or she will accomplish that objective.

Telling the "what" and delegating the "how" offers a growth opportunity to both parties. The employee grows by figuring out how to accomplish the objective. And the manager grows from learning to trust, to lead, to support. Additionally, the manager, through effective delegation, becomes far more productive.

Upward Delegation

More often than you'd think, both manager and employee fall into the trap of "upward delegation." Not knowing how, or not being willing to discover how, to accomplish an objective, the employee might walk into his or her boss's office looking for "help." Bosses who do not handle the situation properly can end up developing the "how" themselves.

That's bad news. Obviously, it keeps employees from growing. Less obviously, it keeps managers from growing, from expanding their ability to accomplish beyond that which they can do with their own head and hands.

Managers should, instead, lead, and counsel the employee. To help without doing the employee's job. To suggest, to support, to trust, to look beyond the immediacy of the task at hand, and to play the game, not the shot.

Selecting Planning Team Members

You'll need to select the individual members of your strategy team. How many people? Oh, perhaps as few as five or six, to as many as ten or twelve. Fewer than five or so and you'll have a difficult time maintaining a high energy level in your strategy sessions. Too many, and your sessions will easily degenerate into tactical, rather than strategic, discussions.

Regarding the selection of your team members, you have two fundamental choices. First, you can take the very traditional approach and select according to the organization chart ... such as all the vice presidents, or all the department managers, or all the branch managers plus all of the department managers. While that method of selection is certainly "politically correct," it generally doesn't result in a team that is best prepared to think strategically.

An alternative approach (but less politically correct, I warn you) is to select team members from various corners of your organization according to one criteria: Is this person a strategic thinker? Yes, I confess, you have to be a bit brave to use this selection method. Because it's less politically correct, you'll be sure to ruffle a few feathers.

"Hey, why was Ernie selected, while I wasn't?

But you know what? You can answer, "Because Ernie has demonstrated that he's a strategic thinker." And that answer will drive home a most important point: That your organization values strategic thinking ... and thus, strategic thinkers.

However you choose your planning team members, make sure they're smart. There is no substitute for intelligence among the management team. No process in the world will substitute for lack of intellect. You'll need visionaries, too. Not everyone has a flair for thinking about the future. Be sure that at least a few of the people on your strategy team possess such flair. That they both enjoy the challenge and are somewhat skilled at future thinking. Or at least they're interested and eager to learn.

CHAPTER 12

BUILDING KNOWLEDGE

IN

YOUR ORGANIZATION

We hear a lot these days about the importance of knowledge – knowledge workers, collective knowledge, institutional knowledge. Here in the 21st century, knowledge is the most important ingredient in business. For in whatever the industry, the knowledgeable organizations are the leading organizations.

But what exactly is knowledge? Where does it come from? And how can you build it up and spread it around your organization?

Step one is *collecting data*. Data are simply recorded inputs, such as stacks of cash register receipts in the grocery store's back office.

Step two is to analyze data in order to convert them to *information*. For example, you can analyze your cash register receipts (the data) to discover how much of each product you sell (the information).

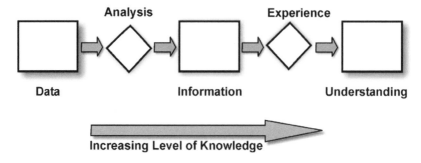

Figure 12 - 1: Building Knowledge

In fact, you really can't communicate data. Imagine trying to present a ten-minute talk about a stack of cash register receipts. In order to communicate your findings, you must first analyze the data, thus converting them into information. Clearly, you could present a ten-minute talk about sales by product, sales by product category, or sales by day of the week – all information obtained by analyzing your data (the cash register receipts).

Having converted data into information, you've increased your level of knowledge. But you'd increase it still further through experience. In step three, as you put the information to use, you arrive at *understanding*.

Having analyzed the cash register receipts (the data), you may learn (the information) that you sell many more red apples than green. But you don't yet know why.

Were you to stand in the produce section of your grocery store observing your customers, you might notice that many of them first reach for a green apple. Then, noting the higher price for green apples, many customers choose the lower-priced red apples. Perhaps you'd couple this observation with your recollection that you sold about as many red apples as green apples when their prices were more similar.

Aha, you've just taken your information, coupled it with experience, and developed an understanding. (Every time someone says "Aha," they've arrived at an understanding.)

Information is knowledge about *what* is happening; understanding is knowledge about *why* it is happening. Understanding (knowing why) is important in a strategic sense. You need to understand (to know why) before you can use knowledge to predict, before you can apply it toward decisions about the future, toward strategies.

Just as you can communicate information, you can also communicate understanding. Just as you can inform a co-worker about your selling more red apples (information), you can also share your *understanding* of your customers' price sensitivity.

This ability to communicate both information and understanding suggests a powerful benefit, a significant point of leverage. Many people – indeed the entire organization – can gain understanding from the experience of a single individual.

Two Significant Challenges

As a leader, you're faced with two significant challenges related to building a knowledge-based organization:

1. How to encourage individual employees to increase their own level of knowledge (successfully moving from data to information to understanding).
2. How to stimulate the entire organization to increase its level of shared knowledge.

The steps required to accomplish both challenges include:

- Model learning. Be inquisitive. Ask, "What is happening?" and, "Why is it happening?" Encourage others to ask similar questions.

- Don't concern yourself so much about immediate answers. Answers may be a while in coming. At least initially, the questions are far more important.
- Discover where the knowledge (data, information and understanding) currently resides in your organization. Map it, or catalog it. Let everyone know to whom they can turn for data, information and understanding.
- Devise systems for apprenticeship, mentoring, and coaching.
- Develop on-going processes to scan for both data (as appropriate) and information (as applicable).
- Make sure that any analysis of data is performed by someone experienced in the applicable subject area. Analysis based on the judgment of an experienced person will produce better information.
- Locate individuals in close physical proximity to encourage informal sharing of information and knowledge.
- In those circumstances where close physical proximity isn't possible (due to dispersed geography or travel), assure that the necessary tools (such as e-mail) are available to encourage on-going dialog.
- Form task teams to get people thinking together.
- Celebrate and reward team efforts. Diminish celebration and reward for individuals alone.
- Welcome – in fact, seek – input from outside the organization.
- Together with your management team, conduct periodic strategy sessions to explore "What's happening?" and "Why?" While you'll likely publish notes from your sessions, your notes won't be your maximum benefit. Instead, your maximum benefit will be the increased level of shared knowledge among your management team members. (Some

years ago, at his division's strategy session, Jim Horner, Engineering Manager for Hewlett Packard's Santa Clara Division remarked, "Even if we forgot to take notes from this session, we'd still have most of the benefit.")

Put 'Em on a Bus

During the mid 1980s, I consulted with Dunn Properties, a commercial real estate development company in Southern California. Bill Brasher, the company's president, discovered one day that his office staff of some 45 – 50 employees didn't fully understand the nature of the company's business. Yes, most of the office staff did know their office procedures and the names of the company's projects. But they lacked any meaningful understanding of those projects. From the receptionist to the book keeper to the director of human resources, all had little awareness of "what life was like" for their fellow-employees "out in the field."

This lack of understanding caused miscommunication between the office staff and those in the field. And as a result, the office staff was doing a rather poor job of supporting their fellow employees.

Believing it was critical for his office employees to know more about the company's projects, Bill closed the office for one day. He hired a temporary receptionist to take phone messages. He rented two buses complete with drivers and loaded all of his office staff aboard the buses. He also rounded up 50 hard hats for the passengers who spent the day touring four of the company's projects across three counties of Southern California.

Upon arriving at each job site, the on-site project manager met the buses and gave the visitors an extensive project tour. The visitors had the opportunity to see the project, and also to ask questions of the project manager and others working at each site. Thus, the office staff acquired a far better understanding of each of the company's projects. Also, the office staff learned about the issues and concerns of those in the field. As a result of this day-long tour, they were better able to relate to, and thus support, their fellow employees in the field.

I recently ran into the same situation with another client. A wholesale distributor ran both a day shift and a night shift in their central warehouse. A total of 37 employees worked those two shifts. Their job was to ship product to the company's 42 sales branches located across three Western States. Here again, those working in the warehouse had little feel for the realities of the business "out in the field" – in this case, out in the sales branches. Because of this lack of understanding, the warehouse personnel were doing a poor job of supporting the sales branches.

Recalling Bill Brasher some years earlier having "put 'em on a bus," I suggested to my wholesale distribution client that he might consider doing the same. While my client is considering my suggestion, he hasn't yet decided whether to "put 'em on a bus." I hope he will.

The important point is that employees must understand the operation of their business if they are to offer significant contribution.

CHAPTER 13

THINKING OUTSIDE THE BOX

W e've all heard the expression, "thinking outside the box." This phrase, as you know, calls for escaping the conventional way of thinking and doing into thinking, and potentially doing, something innovative.

As you also know, thinking outside the box is tough. It's tough because managers are often reluctant to venture from the security of the box, from the security of convention and "the world as they know it." Thinking *inside* the box, on the other hand, easily becomes habit, habit supported by culture. And culture changes ever so slowly, ever so reluctantly.

Depending on the organization's management style, thinking outside the box may even be unwelcome. I recall a client in Los Angeles whose management team was severely reprimanded for departing from the president's strategy of "staying the course." The managers quickly learned that it was far safer to "stay the course" than to suggest doing something different. Clearly, in that organization, it wasn't safe to think outside the box.

Strangely enough, success can also block thinking outside the box. If an organization has been "doing okay" by staying the course, managers might wonder, "Why should we even consider change?" One answer, of course, is that while the organization is "doing okay" today, it might do even better with some outside-the-box thinking, especially when today's world is in rapid flux. So, perhaps an even more significant answer is that while the organization is "doing okay" today, its current strategy may be inappropriate tomorrow.

The final reason why managers are often reluctant to think outside the box is their propensity toward convergent, rather than divergent, thinking. Divergent thinking makes no attempt to decide, but rather introduces a number of different possible choices. Very often, those choices are outside of the box. Convergent thinking "narrows down" among a number of choices – honing in, making a decision. Without intervention, managers – and especially management teams – will generally tend toward convergent thinking

Okay, so how can you encourage managers – and management teams – to think outside the box? Two important ways:

1. Think about the degree to which you're asking managers to think outside the box. Conceptually, it's easier to get them to think outside the box if you promise that, while outside the box, they can "hold one hand on the box." That is, the degree to which you ask them to depart from the box is such that they won't be "floating outside in space." Here, you're offering them some degree of safety by promising to limit the degree of change.

2. To encourage your managers to think outside the box is to demonstrate the importance of doing so. You'll need to show how the world around you is changing and how today's strategy is unlikely to serve you tomorrow. You'll need to get their attention, to "stir the pot."

Figure 13 - 1: One Hand on the Box

Some years ago, I worked with The Harris Group, a consulting engineering firm in Seattle. Terry Valo, then the company's president, foresaw a downturn in the industry. He "painted a picture" of his vision on a flipchart easel. In fact, he convinced his management team to completely redirect the company's marketing strategy. You know what? His prediction turned out to be "right on the money."

Brainstorming

You'll benefit from teaching your management team to think outside the box – to think creatively, divergently. An exercise in brainstorming can work wonders. Here, participants suggest one idea after another in sort of a "free for all" with a few simple rules. The rules are:

- No idea is too crazy. Every idea counts for it just might trigger someone else's "winner" idea.
- Building on someone else's previously mentioned idea is great.
- No criticism of any idea is allowed. Just keep moving.

Another exercise in creativity – my favorite, in fact – is to ask your management team to think up as many uses as they can for a common object, such as a toothpick. Give them ten minutes or so, and see what they come up with. See if they discover a toothpick's use as a cleaning device for small objects such as jewelry. Or as a filler for screw holes in wood. Or an applicator for paint in small places. Or as a device to hold your eye lids open while you're reading a dull novel (remember, no idea is too crazy). They'll have fun and, more importantly, they'll build confidence in their ability to think outside the box.

Back in the 1960s, the world of business was a whole lot more stable, and significantly more predictable than it is today. Companies then could get away with inside-the-box strategies. Not now! In today's more challenging – indeed, less forgiving – business environment, inside-the-box strategies are applicable to far fewer businesses. By tomorrow, or perhaps the day after tomorrow, they'll be applicable to none.

Celebrate Failure

If managers are going to think outside the box – if they're going to try some "far-out stuff" – they've got to expect some failures. For certainly not all of their far out ideas will succeed. Encouraging outside-the-box thinking thus necessitates accepting a fair share of failures.

This tolerance for failure is hard for many managers to accept. Nonetheless, it's necessary for employees to experiment with new, innovative – and necessarily somewhat riskier – ideas.

Some years ago, I worked with a client who fully appreciated the need to accept failure. In fact, he actually threw an after-hours party following the "burial" of each "dead-end idea." Yes, his managers did come up with their fair share of dead-end ideas. But they also came up with more than their fair share of innovative new ideas and newly developed products.

You've likely heard the story about Thomas Edison's response to a reporter's question during his on-going series of attempts to invent the light bulb. The reporter asked, "Aren't you discouraged, Mr. Edison, at your many failures in your attempt to develop the light bulb?"

The great inventor responded, "I haven't failed at all. I've discovered nearly 1,000 ways *not* to build a light bulb."

Yet one more story comes to mind. Babe Ruth, certainly among the greatest homerun hitters of all time, also held the record for strikeouts in a single season. He well understood that to hit the ball at all, and specifically to drive it over the outfield fence, he had to swing. Some of the time – in fact, much of the time – he'd simply miss the ball.

> *"Every strike brings me closer to the next home run."*
> — Babe Ruth

A Sharp Picture of a Fuzzy Concept

As we discussed in Chapter 1, photographer Ansel Adams said, "There is nothing worse than a sharp picture of a fuzzy concept." Also, management guru Peter Drucker offered, "There is nothing more wasteful than becoming highly efficient at doing the wrong thing."

Both Adams and Drucker offered the same message. First be sure you're doing "the right thing." Then – and only then – do that right thing well. Effectiveness (doing the right thing) first, efficiency (doing it well) second. And no, you can't reverse the order of these two steps.

A client I worked with in 1998 is a bright, energetic, young fellow. In fact, he did a wonderful job at efficiently managing a product line for his company. However, due to market conditions, his company simply couldn't make money selling his particular product line.

You see? It didn't matter how wonderfully this fellow performed his job. He could have been absolutely super-efficient. It didn't matter. For he, through no fault of his own, was *doing the wrong thing*. He was managing a product line that simply could not make money for his company.

Keep it Simple

A participant at an American Management Association Strategic Planning Course told of her company's retaining a large accounting / consulting firm to recommend appropriate changes to her organization structure. Seems that the accounting / consulting firm had recommended the addition of two management levels.

The course participant went on to explain that, upon receiving the recommendation, her management team was concerned. They felt that the addition of two levels of management was perhaps more than the organization could comfortably absorb. So they saw it as a risky change. Yes, they'd be willing to make the change, but they'd first have to be convinced it was really necessary.

Without knowing the company's specific situation, I sensed that the management team's response was correct. It seemed to me that, intuitively, the team members knew that digesting two layers of managers would be difficult … and just maybe, might be wrong.

I suggested, "OK, let's suppose that you really do need at least one additional management level. What if you added one layer of managers and waited a while to see how it worked out?

If, after six months or so, you realized that you needed yet another, you could then add the additional level."

The participant said she liked my suggestion and would discuss it with her management team.

So very often, people (including some consultants) jump to the more complex solution. But so very often, it's the simpler solution that's easier and less costly to implement. And often, the simpler is also the better solution.

There's an old saying: "Kiss," which stands for "Keep it simple, stupid." If we're devising a strategy, and we have the choice of erring on the side of simplicity, or erring on the side of complexity, I recommend we err on the side of simplicity. Most often the simpler strategy will work just fine. Also, it will be easier on your resources and easier for your employees to understand. Thus, to support.

And, if after six months or a year, you discover that you really do need to complicate your strategy (like adding another layer of management), you can then do so. Better that than attempting the more complex strategy and setting yourself up for failure.

Shoot the Engineer

In your attempt to keep things simple, you may have to fight with your engineers. In fact, there's an old joke which goes...

> Question: "How many engineers does it take to screw in a light bulb?"
>
> Answer: "It takes two, one to screw in the bulb and the other to tell him when he's finished."

While this old story, like so many old stories, makes use of exaggeration, it also makes a point. So many products (and services) are simply over-designed.

Who says they're over-designed? The customers out there in the marketplace, that's who. Those are the folks who count. In fact, they're the *only* folks who count. For they get to decide which products and services they'll buy.

I once worked with a residential real estate developer in Southern California. The firm had recently developed a new model single-family home for sale in Riverside County. While the initial specification called for the home to be "affordably priced," the design team decided to add a few "extras" such as a more spacious kitchen, upgrades in flooring, and some architectural "niceties." Naturally, these goodies added cost for the developer who then had to raise the selling price of the home. The company ended up with a home somewhat overpriced for the area. Fortunately for the developer, with a bit of time, and with some help from a "hot market," the homes all sold. Not all over-designers are so fortunate. Many end up with an unsaleable product or service.

You'll need to control the development of any new product or service. First find out what your customers want to purchase, and at what price. Then figure out if you can produce the product or service at a low enough cost so you can make an acceptable profit selling at that price. Then communicate those specifications, along with the target production cost, to your design team. And, for goodness sake, manage the project so your design folks develop *to* – rather than *over* – the specifications and the target cost.

Hey, I know what it's like. I have an engineering degree. I've designed my share of products. I know how enticing it is to add just one more little "goodie" to a product or service. Beware however. Bells and whistles can be very, very costly. Consider this question: How much does it cost your company to launch a new product or service? OK, now what if that product or service were to miss its market? What if your customers simply wouldn't purchase your product or service? How much would you lose? Think about it.

SIO

When Dave Hornbaker was vice-president of Trans-Met Engineering Corp, he gave everyone in the organization an anxious week. One weekend, he placed a dozen or so small but conspicuous signs around the company – on his office door, on his secretary's desk, on the bulletin board in the assembly area, on the blackboard in the engineering lab. Each sign carried the same message: "SIO."

On Monday morning, everyone wanted to know, "Why all the signs? And, what do the letters 'SIO' mean?"

Dave offered the same answer to all inquirers. "I'll tell you on Friday," he announced. That week, Dave's drama became the "talk of the office." Just about everyone speculated on the meaning of "SIO." Did it mean "Security in Office"? Or "Succeed in Opportunities"? Or "Similar is Opposite"?

On Friday, Dave called a meeting of all managers. He began that meeting by directing a question to the marketing manager. Dave asked, "Have you ever arrived in a hotel to discover you'd forgotten to pack your pajamas? Or your toothbrush? Or your socks?"

The marketing manager confessed he'd forgotten a thing or two a time or two.

"Why don't you make a checklist of things to pack?" asked Dave. "Then when preparing for a trip, you could refer to your checklist. That way, you'd eliminate the problem of forgetting things. You'd *solve it once*."

And so, the meaning of SIO became clear: *Solve It Once*. The managers spent the next thirty minutes or so offering examples of Dave's SIO philosophy. They should stop "fixing" the worn out milling machine twice each month and, instead, rebuild or replace it. And they should stop fighting the quality problems of a now-ancient product; instead, obsolete the product and replace it. They decided they should stop doing battle with an uncooperative employee – fire him and seek a replacement.

It's amazing how much energy in how many companies goes into "solving" the same old problem – again and again. It's pretty expensive in terms of opportunity lost. Opportunity lost because the company's resources are spent, not really solving, not really accomplishing, and certainly not progressing toward a growth objective.

Worse perhaps, solving the same old problem (again) tends to focus peoples' attention on problems. And focus on problems isn't the way to build a profitable, growing company. You build a profitable, growing company by focusing, not on problems, but on opportunities. You need to make room for that focus on opportunities. You've got to identify the problem, make a decision, solve it once and get on with your opportunities – and get on with profitable growth.

Thanks, Dave.

CHAPTER 14

NOBODY CAN SPRINT
FOREVER

A number of years ago, I was staying in the San Francisco Marriott while teaching an American Management Association Strategic Planning Course. At the end of the first day's class, I returned to my guest room on one of the hotel's upper floors. As I approached the door to my room, I reached into my jacket pocket and took out my room key.

As the Marriott was a modern hotel, the key was an electronic card. I inserted the card into the slot on the door. Oh oh! A red light rather than green. I tried twice more. Still, a red light. The door didn't open.

Hmmm… I figured I'd have to go back down to the reception desk to have my key re-programmed, so I started down the hallway toward the elevator. But suddenly, I stopped, for a new thought had popped into my head. I wondered, "What if I reached into my other pocket and found another key from the Marriott? What if that second key then opened my door? What if the key I tried earlier had been from a previous trip to the same hotel?"

Well, guess what? Yep, you're right. I found a second Marriott key in my other pocket. And yes, it opened the door.

"Man," I thought, "I'm traveling too much. I'm too busy."

I continued to think of myself as "too busy" until a week later when I ran into Jerry at the airport. Now Jerry was *really* too busy.

Jerry and I first met as next door neighbors about thirty years ago. And once in a while, here and there, we run into each other. When we bumped into each other at the airport that morning, we were waiting to board the same flight.

"Hey, Jerry, how are you doing?" I asked.

"Hi, Bill, I'm fine, long time no see," he replied.

"Looks like you and I are on the same flight to Dallas," I added. "Is that your final destination?"

Then a long silence. Jerry thought as he replied, "No, I'm not going to Dallas. I'm going to … ugh … ugh …" After a ten second pause, perhaps longer, he remembered, "I'm going on to Memphis."

It seemed strange that a fellow about to board an airplane couldn't more easily recall his final destination. But Jerry had a great excuse. He was awfully busy. Jerry had a background in engineering, and had become quite the expert in computer software. And back in the 1980s, when Lotus Development Corporation created the Lotus 1-2-3 software package, Jerry became expert in the use of that program. Soon thereafter, Dun and Bradstreet decided to offer public seminars instructing business managers on the use of Lotus 1-2-3 and contracted with Jerry to teach their course. Over time, he mastered additional programs and taught a number of courses for D&B.

Jerry explained, "I generally fly out to some distant city on a Sunday, teach the two-day D&B course on Monday and Tuesday.

Then on Tuesday night, I fly to another city to teach the same course on Wednesday and Thursday. Then I fly home on Thursday night. Last year I did that 45 weeks of the year."

Jerry went on to explain that he'd already logged 130,000 frequent flier miles during the year (it was mid-April). He pulled his itinerary from his pocket. It listed his teaching assignments for the rest of the year (April thru December). His itinerary reached to the floor.

Jerry related that a week earlier he'd been eating dinner in a hotel restaurant. He finished his meal and wrote on his bill, "Charge to Room 1806." He walked to the elevator, stepped inside and reached out to push the button for the eighteenth floor. He couldn't find it. In fact, he discovered that the hotel had only twelve floors. Seems Jerry had, perhaps a week earlier, stayed in room 1806 in another hotel. As his room key didn't have a room number imprinted on it, he walked up to the front desk, identified himself, and asked the desk clerk for his room number. Then he returned to the restaurant to clear up the matter of his dinner bill.

I noticed that Jerry had put on a fair amount of weight. So I asked, "Do you manage to get any exercise?"

"No, just walking from the airplane to ground transportation and pacing back and forth in front of the classroom. When I arrive late at an airport, I immediately call my hotel, knowing the restaurant is soon to close. I ask to speak to the restaurant manager and explain that I'm on my way from the airport. I persuade the restaurant manager to cook a late order for me. Generally, it's salad, soup, steak and lobster. After all, D&B is paying for it, so why shouldn't I treat myself?"

I asked Jerry, "Do you enjoy being so busy?"

"No, I don't find it fun any more. I'm pretty tired of the travel. On Fridays, I do some consulting for local clients. Help a few local firms with their computer systems. But I'm too busy to send a statement. In fact, I haven't billed a client since August. One client said he doesn't want my charges accumulating. So he sends me $1,000 each month. I don't send him a statement or anything."

Aware of my temptation to impose my own value system on Jerry, I went pretty easy with my suggestion. "You know, Jerry, you may have the opportunity to cut back a bit on your teaching and expand your local consulting business."

"Yeah, I know. But teaching the seminar is so lucrative. D&B pays me a basic teaching fee plus an additional amount for each attendee beyond the first ninety or so. I earn about $250,000 a year."

But who cares? What kind of a life is it when a guy lives in ... hey, I almost forgot the most important part of the story – Jerry has a wife and three kids. His kids' ages were then six, seven and ten. As we walked to the plane, he recalled, "Bill, your kids are about the same age as mine, aren't they?"

I replied, "Yes, they are. I've got two boys."

He suggested, "Hey, we're going to have to get our families together." And then he chuckled as he added, "But of course, I'm never home."

Moral of the story – nobody can sprint forever. Don't ever get so busy that you forget to live your life. And don't let your employees do it, either.

PART IV

PROCESS

CHAPTER 15

THE 80 – 20 RULE WORKS ABOUT 80% OF THE TIME

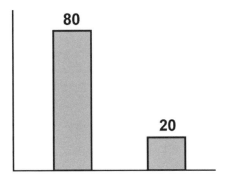

If you're growing a row of flowers, you'll want them all to look pretty. Nice and even. Full bloom, rich color. Water them all. Fertilize evenly. Make sure they all make it.

But if you breed race horses, your strategy is entirely different. You buy a few, breed a few, train them all, until ... until you discover that you have a truly exceptional horse. A winner. Then you pour all of your resources into your winner.

In running your business, you've got a choice. You can manage as if you're raising flowers. Or as if you're raising race horses.

You can invest resources attempting to make the non-bloomers bloom. Get 'em all even. Make sure they all make it. Invest resources in fixing your weak products, your weak markets, your weak employees.

Or you can invest your resources in the winners. In making your fastest horses run still faster. Pour resources on your winning products, your winning markets, your winning employees.

There's a strong tendency to manage your business as if you were growing flowers. To invest resources in an attempt to obtain a similar return on all products, markets and people. This management-by-exception strategy results in a greater investment in lower-performing assets.

Such management-by-exception is *wrong*. For business is a lot more like race horses than flowers. Your strongest products, markets and people are most responsive to the investment of additional resources. That's where you'll find your maximum payback.

So when your marketing guy tells you he's come up with one more idea to revitalize that poor selling product, tell him to forget it. Tell him to spend his time thinking up a way to sell still more of your better-selling products.

Careful though. While it's *generally* correct to apply the 80–20 rule, it isn't always correct. You do know about the 80–20 rule, don't you? It's been around for quite some time …

Vilfredo Pareto (Italy, 1848-1923) developed The Law of Maximum Ophelimity. Today, that hard-to-pronounce law is more commonly known as Pareto's Law or, simply, "the 80–20 rule." Briefly stated, the law claims that "80% of the output comes from 20% of the input."

While Pareto's fields were economics and sociology, his law also applies to the world of business. For example, 80% of profit generally comes from 20% of the products or services offered. Figure it out for your own business. It fits, doesn't it?

And, 80% of quality problems come from 20% of the components, sub-systems or suppliers. They're the recurring problems that managers "solve" over and over.

The law works for people, too. Eighty percent of your employee problems come from 20% of your employees. Close your eyes and you'll see those employees standing before you. About 20%, right?

And money, too. Of total dollar expense, 80% goes to 20% of the expense categories. You can check this one quickly. Just glance at your income statement.

Did I generalize in each of these examples? Sure I did. But more often than not, each is true. The 80–20 rule works pretty darn well as a "rule of thumb" in many areas of the business world.

The strategy for managing such 80–20 situations is simple. Focus on managing the 20% of input accounting for 80% of output. Push the 20% of products and services that yield 80% of profit. Work on the 20% of components, sub-systems and suppliers that cause 80% of quality problems. Redirect or replace the 20% of your employees who cause 80% of your headaches. Be watchful of the 20% of expense categories accounting for 80% of total dollar expense.

But be careful. You can't always manage by the 80–20 rule. Because it doesn't always apply.

It doesn't apply when events are *linked* rather than independent, i.e., when an event is dependent upon the one that preceded it. In those cases, not just 80%, but 100% of those linked events must be managed successfully.

It's like traveling from Los Angeles to Boston by plane. First you drive your car to Los Angeles airport. After parking in the long-term lot, you hop aboard the courtesy bus which hauls you off to terminal four. You board your plane, sit back to watch a movie, and a few hours later you land at Boston's Logan Field.

There you pick up your rental car for a thirty minute drive to your suburban hotel.

Think about the trip you just completed. You spent about 80% of your travel time aboard the airplane. Certainly you covered well over 80% of the mileage by plane. And spent about 80% of your travel expense on the plane as well. But that doesn't mean you need manage only that (80%) portion of your trip. You must manage *every single* leg of the trip right down to the airport parking lot courtesy bus whose six minute, mile and one eighth ride we all take for granted. The events are linked. Each must be successful if the whole process (getting from Los Angeles to Boston) is to be successful.

In the business world, many projects require the successful completion of *each* of a number of linked events. For example, when executing a contract, you must select the contracting party, develop the terms and conditions of contract, and make the proposal. Then you must consider the other party's counter-proposal. Then analyze. And negotiate. Then you shake hands. Then explain the whole thing to your attorney. Then explain to the other party's attorney. Draw up the contract and explain to the attorney again. Then draw up the contract again. Then sign the contract and get the other party to sign the contract. Then shake hands again. Then do what you promised to do in the contract.

You can't do just 20% of these steps right. Because *all* of the events are linked. Each one depends on those preceding it. You've got to manage all 100%.

Consider the hiring of a key employee. You've got to search for the right person, contact him, interview him, ask questions, answer questions, think about it, ask some more questions, answer some more questions, think about it some more, develop and present an offer, wait, consider his counter-offer, negotiate, shake hands, and finally write a letter of confirmation. Again, you can't manage 20% of the steps. You've got to work on all 100%.

Think about developing a new product or service. You first identify a market need. Test it for a match with your internal capabilities. Commit the resources to develop the product or service. Begin development. Continue development. Keep continuing development. Test the new product or service in the marketplace. Redesign. Re-test. Design the market introduction program. Complete all drawings and manuals. Release to production. Release to distribution. And introduce to the market. Again, you've got to manage the whole 100%. The 80–20 rule doesn't work here either.

The 80–20 rule is a useful tool to carry around in your managerial tool kit. It works in a whole bunch of places. Use it where you can. But don't overdo it! Because, like any other tool, it doesn't always apply.

"If the only tool you have is a hammer, you tend to see every problem as a nail."

— Abraham Maslow

Applying Pareto's Law

Some years ago, I worked with a San Diego company which assembled plastic blood bags, intravenous feeding bags and medical tubing. They sold their products to hospitals in the United States and Canada.

Their customer list numbered well over 200 hospitals, but only a handful of those customers accounted for any significant sales volume. In fact, their largest two customers provided just over 55% of the company's sales. Clearly, the company was over-dependent on those two accounts, and the company's management team was justifiably concerned about this situation.

A second issue came to light during the company's strategy sessions. It turned out that, among the company's 200+ customers, most represented such a tiny fraction of the company's sales – and worse yet, ordered product in such very small quantity – that the company actually lost money selling to those accounts.

So while the over-dependence on two large accounts suggested that the company should focus on others, the numerous (money-losing) smaller accounts suggested that, the company do exactly the opposite and continue to focus on a few larger accounts. Management seemed torn between these two competing issues.

In working with the management team, I suggested we make use of the Pareto diagram. That is, we plot sales by customer so we'd get a visual feel for the "dilemma" that the company faced. The diagram clearly showed the company's dependence on the two top accounts. (See Figure 15 - 2.)

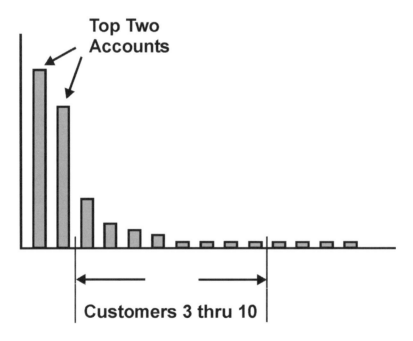

Figure 15 - 2: Sales by Customer

I suggested the company work at increasing total sales to the third through the tenth largest accounts. This objective would focus management's attention on increasing sales to eight significant customers without the dilution of attention on many (potentially 200) smaller accounts.

As it turned out, sales to customers 3 through 10 was, at the time, running 26% of total sales. The management team adopted this suggestion, and set a quantified objective calling for increasing that number to 40% within two years. Naturally, the company didn't pursue its objective by turning away additional business from its two largest accounts. Instead, it developed accounts ranking 3 –10 to balance any increase in business from the two largest accounts. Also, management became very selective about accepting business from smaller, less profitable accounts.

This objective, and the focus it brought to the sales effort, served the company well. Within two years, the company had raised total sales to customers 3 – 10 to 44% of total sales while increasing the company's total sales by 71%. Total dollar sales from the company's top two accounts actually rose. But because of the greater increase in sales to customers 3 through 10, the top two customers accounted for just 43% of total sales.

Because of its well-focused sales strategy, the company increased total sales while reducing dependence on its two top accounts. Also, because of re-directing its focus from "all 200 accounts" to the more profitable customers 3 through 10, total profit increased significantly.

CHAPTER 16

GET THE LEAD OUT!

To prosper in a tough economic environment, business leaders must make some difficult decisions. Those decisions will set the stage, not only for surviving the inevitable cyclical downturns, but also for sustaining growth during economic recoveries.

In responding to a weakening economy, there are two fundamental kinds of money-saving strategies managers can choose. First, they can chop expenses, which typically means cutting controllable expenses such as marketing and employee training, or laying off employees.

While chopping expenses does provide savings in the short term, those short-term savings come at a very high price. Cutting marketing expenses, for example, often leads to a decrease in sales some six or eight months "downstream." Bad enough if the economy soon turns up. At least the boost from an improving economy might then mask the company's weakened competitive position. But what if the economic downturn were to last another year or more? Having cut marketing expenses could then prove fatal.

Cutting employee training is also an expensive "savings." For it's a sure way to fall behind the productivity curve in a competitive environment. As for layoffs, this "last resort," short-term strategy comes with morale problems, plus later hiring and training expenses, as well. And once again, productivity suffers. Indeed, chopping expenses hardly seems a way to "play the game, not the shot."

The second type of money-saving strategy is far more beneficial in the long term. That strategy is to "get the lead out!" Yes, I know this calls for an explanation. Here it comes ….

Every organization – some more than others – is burdened by dead weight. What do I mean by dead weight? I mean a lack of focus in its many dimensions. Like too many products and services, some of which aren't pulling their weight in profit contribution. Or too many product options adding layers of complexity and inefficiency.

Some years ago, I worked with a client on an analysis of both sales revenue and profit contribution for each of the products the company manufactured. To management's surprise, a full 37% of the company's products (representing 14% of the company's sales revenue) offered negative contribution to profit. Following the analysis, the company's management team "killed" a number of unsuccessful products. They "got the lead out" and profits quickly improved, not just from the elimination of "dead weight" products, but also from management's greater level of focus on those stronger, remaining products. (See Figure 16 - 1.)

Many companies have a number of "wrong" customers. Those companies are so driven by sales volume that they never stop to analyze whether particular customers are really contributing to bottom-line profit. So they continue to serve unprofitable customers.

I worked with a client on an analysis of both sales revenue and profit contribution by customer. Our findings were an eye-opener for the management team. We discovered that four customers, representing 13% of the company's sales revenue, were actually contributing negative profit! Again, the company's man-

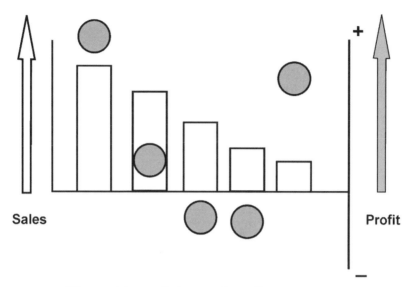

Figure 16 - 1: Sales and Profit by Product

agement team "got the lead out." Actually, they let just one customer go. They turned two others profitable through pricing strategy. They turned the fourth profitable through changing the product mix.

Any time is a good time to "get the lead out" of your business but during an economic downturn, that's a *great* time!

The Fat Curve

Here's an important lesson from recent history. Early in 1984, *The Wall Street Journal* reported results of the WSJ/Gallup survey of 822 top U.S. executives. That survey questioned the executives on their feeling about the recession of 1981-1982, which had then recently ended. Guess what? Seven out of ten thought the recession was a good thing for the country!

The surveyed executives said, "It was a well justified adjustment." "Perhaps it was the medicine we needed." "It put a dose of reality into our lives – sharpened us up."

Well let's reflect on the specific lessons learned from recessions. Just how do recessions "sharpen us up"?

Surely, many of the 822 surveyed executives were from companies that had layoffs during the recession. OK, whom did they lay off? Good people or deadwood? If deadwood, why in the world wasn't that deadwood booted out *before* the recession?

Surely, a number of the 822 executives narrowed product lines during the recession – discontinued products and services that weren't quite making it. Focused, instead, on the "real winners." Then why, before the recession, were they hanging on to the "real losers"?

I could go on to ask about tolerance for unprofitable activities, belated make-versus-buy decisions, and mismanaged marketing programs. But I won't. I've already made my point – that during a recession, things get so terrible that business managers finally stop doing the things they never should have been doing in the first place.

Managing their business in times of non-recession, executives have their choice. They can hang on to a few weaker products and services, a few marginal activities, a "monument to management" here and there. They can put on a few extra inches around the middle management.

Or, they can act the way they're forced to act during the recession. They can run lean and insist on *winners only*.

Why should they run lean? Two reasons:

1. That's how to grow profitably when times are good.
2. That's how to remain prepared for times which aren't so good.

"Companies don't get in trouble during the bad times.
They get in trouble during the good times."

– Thomas Watson, founder of IBM

What About Quality?

While in San Francisco teaching the American Management Association's Strategic Planning Course, I had a fascinating conversation. Attending the course was Jon Ragaz, who at the time, was director of Marketing for Alta Dena Dairy.

After the first day's class, Jon and I got into one of those really "fun" conversations. You know, one of those fast-paced dialogs where we were not only talking to each other, but drawing diagrams at the same time.

The subject of our discussion was quality, and Jon made a very interesting, though perhaps controversial, point. He said, "You can't sell Total Quality Control to Americans."

"What do you mean?" I asked.

Jon explained, "You can't sell Total Quality Control to Americans because we Americans don't like the word 'total,' we don't like the word 'quality,' and we don't like the word 'control.' We don't like the word 'total' because it's too extreme for us. It smacks of totalitarianism and goes against our middle-of-the-road preference. We don't like the word 'quality' because, historically at least, we've run into the word only when quality was sub-par. Something was wrong. We were in trouble. As a result, we're somewhat afraid of the word 'quality.' And, finally, we don't like the word 'control' because our independent, individualistic nature guarantees our discomfort with that word."

How interesting! I'd never before thought of the semantic problem related to Total Quality Control.

I followed up on Jon's point by explaining my equally unconventional view on quality. In fact, I drew a diagram. The horizontal axis of my diagram represents the level of quality of any particular product or service. Naturally, an increasing level of quality corresponds to an increasing cost of supplying such quality.

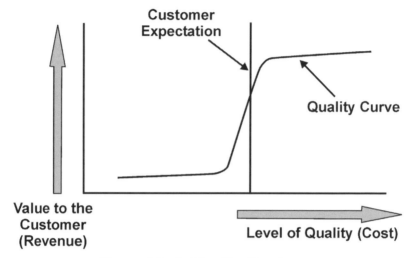

Figure 16 - 2: The Quality Curve

The vertical axis represents value to the customer. Naturally, an increasing value to the customer corresponds to an increasing revenue for the company providing the product or service.

On my chart, a particular vertical line represents the customer's (the market's) expectation of quality.

Now look at the quality vs. value (cost vs. revenue) curve. Note that value to the customer (revenue) increases as level of quality (cost) increases. Pretty much as you'd expect. Note, too, that value to the customer (revenue) remains very low when level of quality is below customer expectation.

However, once the level of quality approaches the customer's expectation, then even a slight increase in quality (cost) creates a significant increase in value to the customer (revenue).

Once above the customer's expectation, however, the cost-revenue relationship changes significantly. Specifically, once above the customer's expectation, additional increases in the level of quality (cost) cause smaller and smaller increases in value to the customer (revenue). So that a company offering a level of quality significantly above their customer's expectation is, in effect, wasting money.

However, we must recognize that the customer's expectation of quality isn't necessarily static. For many products and services, it's dynamic. For example, we've come to expect that the quality of automobiles will increase from year to year. On my model, the automobile buyer's expectation line will move further and further to the right. So providers of automobiles are challenged to continually increase the quality of their offerings.

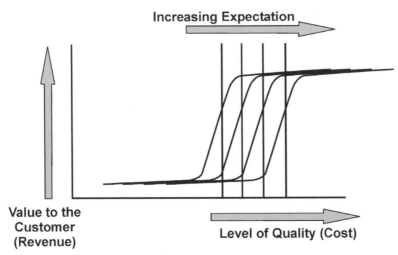

Figure 16 - 3:
Increasing Customer Expectation of Quality

One more important point: If your customer's expectation of quality is to increase, you'd like for it to be your products and services that drive such increase. You'd like to be "out in front of the pack." Certainly, you would not like to be *behind* the quality curve.

CHAPTER 17

KEEP YOUR EYE ON PRODUCTIVITY

I recently spoke with a company president about his being caught in a difficult "cost squeeze." It seems that his product pricing was relatively inflexible due to intense competitive pressure. At the same time, his employee expenses continued to march ever upward based on salary increases and significantly higher medical insurance premiums. So if his product sales this year were the same as last, he'd actually make less money than he did a year ago. Thus the cost squeeze. (See Figure 17 - 1.)

I asked him if he'd been measuring sales per employee. He said he had and that sales per employee had been running about $500,000 per year during the last few years. I suggested that he implement strategies to increase this number significantly. For increasing productivity – specifically, sales per employee – could be his solution to the cost squeeze.

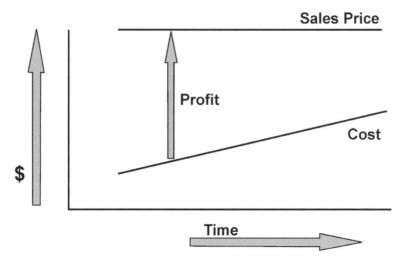

Figure 17 - 1: The Cost Squeeze

We discussed the four fundamental ways he might increase productivity:

- Eliminate "dead weight"
- Use technology to improve systems and processes
- Build employee enthusiasm
- Transfer labor to the buyer.

1. Eliminate "Dead Weight"

As we discussed earlier (see Chapter 16, "Get the Lead Out!"), every organization suffers, to some degree, from a lack of focus. Like offering too many products or services, some of which aren't earning a profit. Or too many product options adding both complexity and inefficiency.

Also, many companies serve a number of "wrong" customers, some of which actually contribute negatively to profit. Companies overly driven by volume don't stop to analyze whether particular customers are really contributing to bottom-line profit. So they continue to serve unprofitable customers.

There are "dead weight" activities, "dead weight" processes, and "dead weight" employees. Find them and get rid of them.

2. Use Technology to Improve Systems and Processes

The second method of improving productivity is through the use of technology – technology in both the factory and in the office. Whether a computer-controlled milling machine or a computerized billing system, technology offers the opportunity for a worker to accomplish more in the same period of time.

For example, FedEx dropped their cost for a package tracking request from $2.14 when handled by a call-center representative to *4 cents* on its web site! While the FedEx savings is certainly more dramatic than that of most companies, it does serve to underscore the possibilities afforded by the appropriate use of technology.

Occasional economic downturns notwithstanding, technology continues to drive gains in productivity. In fact, as economic downturns tend to cap prices, and thus aggravate the cost squeeze, increasing productivity through system and process improvements actually becomes more important during such downturns.

3. Build Employee Enthusiasm

No matter what your strategy for productivity improvement, you'll do a far better job of implementing that strategy if your employees work enthusiastically. For more than anything else, strategy implementation depends on the degree to which your employees care.

But they won't care unless you show them *why* they should care. So, you'd better tell them what's important and why. Some years ago, Larry Potter, Division Manager for Hewlett Packard's Manufacturing Systems Division, told his management team, "Our employees are ready to be passionate; it's up to us to tell them what to be passionate about." Larry's right. And his message underscores the importance of communicating a compelling strategic vision for the organization.

A vision of making more profit, believe it or not, isn't important enough, for it isn't a big enough cause. Instead, your vision must be bigger than you and your employees. When John Kennedy spoke of "landing a man on the moon and returning him safely to earth," he communicated a large, grandiose vision. You must do the same.

Offer your employees a voice in their workplace. Delegate as much as practical. Their feeling of empowerment will encourage them to contribute far more than ever before. Also, you'll find that your controlling less and delegating more allows you to accomplish, through others, far more. And isn't this leveraging the workforce what sound management is really all about?

4. Transfer Labor to the Buyer

The fourth fundamental way to increase productivity often goes unnoticed but it's actually quite significant. It's the transfer of labor from seller to buyer. Yes, you're familiar with this transfer of labor. Think about the food market. Back fifty or sixty years ago, a customer walked into her local "ma and pa" grocery store and found either ma or pa standing behind the service counter. The customer then asked ma or pa for a particular product. As grocery products were then stacked on shelves behind the counter, ma or pa took the product down from the shelf and placed it on the counter. Only with the coming of supermarkets in the 1950s did the *customer* begin to take products from the shelf. This was the beginning of self-service. In an economic sense, self-service transferred labor from seller to buyer.

Following the Arab oil embargo of 1973, we saw a similar transfer of labor from seller to buyer at the gas station. We then began to pump our own gasoline. Self-service restaurants also transfer labor from seller to buyer. In each of these examples – supermarket, filling station and self-service restaurant – the seller is able to increase productivity by reducing his labor content.

And think about this – technology also helps to transfer labor from seller to buyer. That's why banks install ATM machines and retailers offer on-line sales.

The message in all of this is – Whatever your business, continue to increase productivity. Look for ways to do so through:

- Eliminating "dead weight"
- Using technology to improve your systems and processes
- Building your employees' enthusiasm
- Transferring labor to your buyer.

CHAPTER 18

WORK A PROCESS

About thirty-five years ago, Richard Goedl was just beginning his career as a sales agent with State Farm Insurance. And one day, way back then, Rich turned up with a revelation. Seems he attended one of those "how to sell" programs that insurance companies are forever holding for their salesmen. There he learned, "Work a process, not a project."

The meaning of that revelation was that, to be a successful insurance salesman, he'd have to look upon his business as an on-going process of prospecting for clients and closing sales. A "continuum" rather than a series of singular deals. The lesson suggests that one shouldn't get bogged down in the specific details of a single deal. Rather, keep "hunting down" a continuous stream of new deals. Over and over. Work a process.

The lesson seemed to make sense to Rich. And it certainly worked fine for him because, by "working a process and not a project," Rich built a thriving insurance practice.

And I guess the lesson made sense to me, too, because I still remember it after all these years. In fact, I think of Rich's lesson often. But you know what? That lesson isn't a universal truth. In fact, the success of the application of that lesson depends largely on the nature of the activity to which it's applied. Examples? Sure …

As in Rich's case, insurance sales lends itself to working a process. The successful insurance agent knows that "it's a numbers game." If he makes enough sales calls, statistically, he'll make enough sales. He works a process.

Retail stores work a process, as well. They cater to a large number of shoppers, none of whom individually contribute a significant portion of the store's total income. In fact, retailers, particularly those in major cities and suburbs, typically don't even know their customers' names. They work a process.

Mail order companies also work a process. They send out hundreds of thousands of catalogs looking for that small, but statistically significant, percentage they need to make the mailing worthwhile. Again, each individual customer represents a very small percentage of the firm's total revenue. The company is working a process.

Other businesses work a project, rather than a process, such as insurance companies that insure large, unique assets like the Empire State Building, Delta Airline's fleet of jets, or the San Diego Zoo. Here, the asset is so large and so unique that the company must manage a special project in creating a unique insurance policy.

The same thing applies to mainframe computers. Each might cost one or two million dollars. Only a few hundred might be sold in any particular year. Each sale is unique because each installation is specific to a particular customer's requirement. The sale and configuration of the mainframe computer can be thought of as a specific project.

Some years ago, I worked with a company that manufactures landing gear for military and commercial airplanes. You've got more fingers than that company has customers. But each of those very few customers represents a very significant percentage of the company's total revenue. Each specific contract calls for a unique combination of specifications, pricing, delivery, and sales strategy. Each is clearly a project.

Many businesses require the management of both process and project. Typically, management of the process will "lead" to the management of specific projects. We find this combination applicable in selling high value-added goods and services. For example, take Rolls Royce automobiles. If you were operating a Rolls Royce dealership, you'd probably begin your sales efforts by managing a process. Perhaps you'd send a mailer (a first class letter) to the affluent folk in your geographic area. But just as soon as Mr. Albert Affluent responds to your mail campaign, you'll "work" old Albert as a project. Project Albert.

The same thing is true in selling investment opportunities (high priced ones), legal services and consulting services.

In each case, the process represents the "finding" of the prospective customer (or client). And the project represents the conversion of the prospect into a customer (or client). And also the delivery of product or service – such as a Rolls Royce with a custom paint job – is a project.

Managing processes requires a different set of skills than managing projects. And typically, the same people won't do an equally good job at both. Those who do well in managing a process have what I call a "horizontal focus." They enjoy doing the same thing over and over again, Fine-tuning the process to make it better and better. Like selling life insurance policies, or running a mail order business or retail store.

Those who do well at managing a project have what I call a "vertical focus." They get their kicks from deep involvement in one or a few projects. Such as selling three insurance policies per year –for the Empire State Building, for Delta's fleet of jets, and for the San Diego Zoo.

Each of your managers, as individuals, tends toward one orientation or the other. Horizontal or vertical. Process or project. And they become uncomfortable in the other mode. The horizontal folk (with a process orientation) become impatient with the details of major projects. And the vertical folk (with a project orientation) become bored with the sameness of an on-going process.

And that's fine. You simply need to recognize which orientation each specific function of your business calls for. And also recognize the fundamental orientation of each of your key employees. And make sure the two match.

Playing Stud Poker

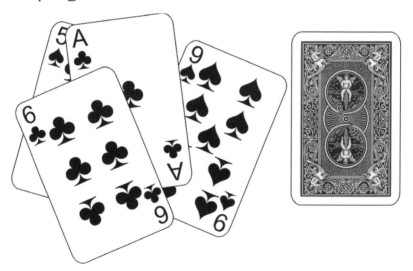

When I was in high school, the guys and I played quite a bit of stud poker. It's an exciting game for 4 to 8 players. It works this way: on the first round, the dealer gives two cards to each player, one face down, the other face up. Each player gets to look at his "down card" but is careful not to show it to the other players. A round of betting follows in which the person with the highest "up card" makes the initial bet. Then, in turn, each player can "call" (match the bet), raise (increase the bet) or drop out.

Following this first round of betting, the dealer gives another card, face up, to each player who hasn't dropped out. Again, a similar round of betting follows. This dealing, followed by a round of betting, occurs four times, until each player still in the game has his initial down card and four up cards.

The object of the game is to hold the highest hand. In increasing order of wonderfulness, hands are: high card, single pair, two pair, three of a kind, straight (five cards in continuous numerical order), flush (five cards of the same suit), four of a kind, and straight flush (five cards of the same suit and in numerical order).

Okay, so here's the most fascinating thing about the game. It's that the betting gets higher and higher with each progressive card dealt. It's relatively cheap to stay (to "call," or match the bet) after the second and even the third card. It's often quite a bit more expensive to stay after the fourth card. And it's generally quite costly to stay on the final round of betting – after the fifth card is dealt.

Here's why. In his first two cards dealt, a player hopes to have a pair or at least a high card "in the hole" (face down). If he has, he wants to encourage others to stay (rather than drop out), so he can win more money on the four rounds of betting. And those players who have less than a high card "in the hole" are staying on speculation. They hope to improve their hand with their cards yet to be dealt. Thus the betting is small.

But on successive rounds, those with a "good" hand, begin to increase the betting so as to win more money. And those who hope to "bluff" others out of the game (betting high on a poor hand in an attempt to convince others that their hand is good) will raise the bet. So each successive round of betting gets more and more costly.

Okay, so now you're wondering, "What in the heck does all of this have to do with the world of business?" Great question! It turns out that projects and processes in the world of business are very much like a game of stud poker. Just as stud poker becomes more and more expensive with each successive card, so does a project and so does a process.

As an example, let's suppose your company is about to launch a new product. Envision the development steps involved. From conceptual design, to full design, to prototyping, to pilot production, to production. You see? A greater financial risk with each step.

Now picture the steps in market research necessary to launch the new product. You might begin with some casual conversation with your existing customers. Little risk here. More formal market research, a far more expensive step, might follow. And your actual launching of the product to the market, your highest risk of all (just like betting after receiving your fifth card).

Consider the process of fixing a quality problem in one of your products. If you catch the problem early – such as way back in the design stage, it's often relatively easy (and inexpensive) to fix. If the product gets as far as the factory floor, and you fix it there, that's quite a bit more expensive. If you catch it at final inspection, more expensive yet. And if you fix the problem after the customer has discovered it, that problem has cost you still a whole lot more.

In creating this book, adding a new paragraph when the manuscript is in a word-processor is trivial. But once the book has been laid out in 6-by-9 format, that change will ripple down through the chapter, requiring each page to be laid out over again. Once the metal printing plates have been created, such a change is very expensive, and once 10,000 copies have been printed, impossibly exorbitant.

Here's the point ... as you move from step to step in both your projects and your processes, you'll need to be confident that you're on the right track. For learning that you're wrong and having to "drop out" at successively later steps becomes far more costly.

"Be sure you're right, then go ahead."

— Daniel Boone

(Speaking of Daniel Boone, did you know that a news reporter once asked the great explorer if he'd ever been lost in the wilderness? Boone replied, "Lost? No, I've never been lost. Once I was confused for three days, but I've never been lost.")

CHAPTER 19

SUCCESSFUL NEW PRODUCTS AND SERVICES

About three years ago, I worked with a mid-sized, West Coast manufacturer who reported a consistently poor history of new product introduction. I soon discovered the reason – the company's new products were a poor fit with its existing products.

This company wasn't alone, by the way. Estimates of the percentage of new products and services that fail run as high as 80%. A disappointingly large number.

You'd think a far greater percentage would succeed, wouldn't you? After all, the majority of new products and services are launched by otherwise successful companies. Companies operating profitable businesses and offering on-going, successful lines of products and services.

And most often, companies launching new products and services commit significant resources. They make use of market research. Invest in capital equipment. And employ intelligent, hard-working people.

And yet their new products and services frequently fail.

They fail for a variety of reasons. Often, they fail because of unfavorable trends in the marketplace, such as tough competition or changing customer preferences. Or they fail because of some violent external event, such as economic turbulence, a war in the Middle East, or government regulation (or deregulation) of a particular industry.

But more often, their failure is caused by some far less violent *internal* factor. Often the new product or service simply *doesn't fit* the organization attempting to launch it. It doesn't fit in one of three specific dimensions. The three dimensions of failure are most often:

- Marketing
- Operations
- Technology.

I explained the situation to my client by drawing two triangles. For each triangle, the three corners represent: "marketing," "operations" and "technology." (See Figure 19 - 1.)

Imagine that Triangle "A" represents the company's existing product line, and Triangle "B" represents the company's new product. We might ask, "How different is the second triangle from the first?" If each corresponding corner of the triangles were located in *exactly* the same place, the new product would be nothing more than an extension of the firm's current product line.

If the "marketing" corner of Triangle B were displaced from that of Triangle A, that would represent a similar product (same

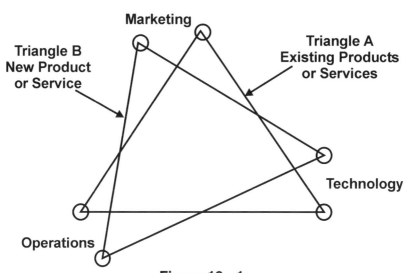

Figure 19 - 1:
Relationship between New and
Existing Products and Services

technology and operations) targeted at a new market. A small displacement of the "marketing" corner represents targeting a *related* market; a larger movement, targeting an *unrelated* market. If the lower right corner were displaced, that would represent a new technology. The lower left corner, new operations.

Now let's ask the big question: "For the launch of a new product, how many corners of the triangle are you attempting to move? And by how much are you attempting to move each of those corners?" In effect, how different is the new product from your existing product in marketing, in technology and in operations?

Generally, organizations can handle a new product that is different from the old in one dimension only. That is, you'd expect a pretty good chance of success if only one corner of the triangle must shift to accommodate a new product. You'd be especially confident if you needed to shift that corner by only a small amount. That would indicate that the new product would be closely related to the old.

Perhaps your organization could handle a change in two dimensions. You'd stand a reasonable chance of success if both of the changes were small – if the new product were related, rather than unrelated to your current products.

But, if you attempt to move two corners of the triangle a significant distance, or to move *all three* corners of the triangle, you're probably asking for trouble. For then, you'd be trying to operate a *very different business* along with your more traditional business.

And guess what happens? Because your more traditional business is just that – more traditional, the new product is just different enough that it represents a "no fit" situation. Though significant, the resources (marketing, technology and operations) you dedicate to the new product are insufficient – or more often, inappropriate – and the new product dies.

And it isn't just product manufacturers that face this problem. We in service organizations do, too. If we simply think of "technology" as "expertise," and "operations" as "delivery of service," we find the argument works just as well for new services as it does for new products.

And it works for new acquisitions, also. If you're interested in buying a company making a similar product in a similar factory, and selling that product to a similar market, you stand a pretty good chance of success. But suppose you're considering acquisition of a firm making a different type of product, using a different manufacturing process, and selling that product to a significantly different market. At the very least, that acquisition will present you with a significant challenge.

Two Organizational Options

Following the logic of this triangular model, you might conclude that companies shouldn't launch significantly different new products or services. That is, you'd expect success only with marginal changes – a relatively small repositioning of only one or two triangle corners. But, as you know, some companies have remarkable success in launching new products and services that are substantially different from their core products and services. How do they achieve this success?

They achieve this success by organizing appropriately. The trick is to set up another division, or operation, or subsidiary, to launch and then manage, the new product or service. In 1981, IBM introduced their new IBM PC, the company's first entry into the personal computer market. They did so by setting up a separate operation 1,800 miles from IBM headquarters. The company's senior managers understood that a start-up PC development / marketing team would be stifled by Big Blue's Big Iron (mainframe) mentality in Armonk, New York. So they sent the start-up team to a distant facility in Boca Raton, Florida.

The two diagrams below (see Figure 19 - 2) show the two ways which you can organize for significant diversification in product or service. The one on the left is the wrong way to organize. The one on the right is the right way to organize. Do you see the difference? Think about it for a moment.

The diagram on the left has a larger box at the top and the smaller boxes at the bottom. This represents a big, strong, boss person overseeing two diverse product (or service) lines and making all of the strategic decisions. Managers of lesser responsibility or lesser capability, or both, report to the big boss. Two problems here:

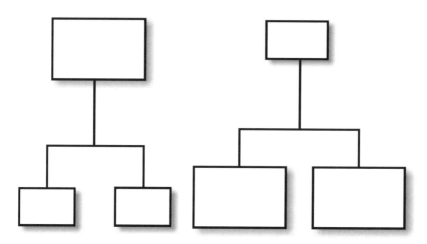

Figure 19 - 2: Two Organizational Options

1. A person of lesser responsibility or lesser capability gets to manage each of the product lines. This is, obviously, less than optimal.
2. The boss person gets to stay awake at night worrying about running two (or more) diverse businesses. Again, this is problematic.

The diagram on the right shows a smaller box at the top and the larger boxes at the bottom. This represents a boss person at the top delegating responsibility to product line (or division) managers – each responsible for a separate (diverse) line of products or services. Big boxes at the bottom of the diagram – big, strong managers, fully responsible for their individual (and each diverse from the other) lines of products or services.

I once worked with a Southern California entrepreneur. This fellow made a small fortune in real estate development during the Southern California's boom years of the 1970s. So far so good.

But because he had a knack for real estate development, he assumed he'd be equally expert at *any* business. So he bought a number of diverse businesses – two gold mines, a resort hotel, a newspaper, a camera manufacturing company and a manufacturer's representative organization. Those businesses were spread across the Southwestern United States, from California to Texas.

To run each of his businesses, he hired a person who was a very good "number two man." That is, because the entrepreneur was "into control," he wouldn't hire a "big, strong" manager, but rather someone who would willingly execute his (the owner's) orders. And then, this particular multi-millionaire got the opportunity to fly around on airplanes, scurrying from one business to another, trying to solve problems which he didn't fully understand. It took him a few years to figure out that this way of life was unworkable. As soon as he endured all the frustration he could handle, he sold all of his businesses. Except one, of course – his real estate development company.

Here again, Bob Stermer's lesson comes to mind: "First-rate people hire first-rate people, second-rate people hire third-rate people."

Chapter 20

Planning For Profit on Smaller Orders

In 1978, I began working for Beckman Instruments' Microelectronics Operation. Almost immediately, I noticed something strange about the organization's pricing strategy. When a customer ordered a number of units of a particular microelectronic device, Beckman would sell the product at a per unit price largely independent of quantity. That is, if Beckman charged $150 apiece for 50 units, it also charged $150 apiece for just 5 units. Oh, maybe they'd offer a 10% discount for quantity. Or charge a small setup fee for low quantity. But for all practical purposes, the per-unit price was pretty much independent of quantity.

This bothered me, for as I looked around the operation, I recognized many costs that seemed independent of order size. Rather, those costs – many difficult to quantify – seemed to be associated with transaction of the order, whatever its size. Thus, smaller orders actually incurred higher per-unit costs.

For example, someone sold the order. Someone entered and scheduled the order for production. Someone ordered the materials and components necessary to build the product. And if the order were late, someone answered the call from an irate customer. Each of these transactions incurred largely the same cost whether the order were for five pieces or for fifty. Thus some costs should have been allocated to the order rather than to each individual unit sold.

Much concerned about this situation, I decided to develop a quantified model to "capture" these per-order costs that escape conventional cost accounting methods.

And so, early in 1979, I developed my "Milk Truck Model." I called it that because I originally used the analogy of a milk truck delivering bottles of milk to houses. I argued that there were certain costs associated with the driver and truck that were best allocated to each stop (at a customer's doorstep) rather than to each bottle of milk.

A couple of years later, then in my own consulting practice, I began teaching at the University of California – Irvine's Extension Program. There, in a course I developed for UCI entitled, "Managing for Growth in the Smaller Company," I introduced my students to my Milk Truck Model. Needing a name for this method of analysis, I called it "Transactional Cost Analysis." I called it that because the analysis was actually based on allocating costs to transactions (the sales order, the stopping of the milk truck at a customer's door step, the receipt of a load of laundry, checking a guest into a hotel, etc.).

In 1985, I finally got around to publishing my method of analysis. In the March–April issue of my *Business Strategies Newsletter*, I presented my Transactional Cost Analysis in an article entitled, *Planning for Profit on Smaller Orders*.

Then, in 1990, when my book *If Your Strategy is So Terrific, How Come it Doesn't Work?* (AMACOM, 1990) was published, my 1985 article found its way into that book's Chapter 39.

All along the way, I'd occasionally introduce the concept to clients as the need arose. Some used it; some didn't.

Then, during the mid-1990s, business managers began talking about a remarkable new method of analysis called, "Activity Based Costing." Sounded important. And people began attending all-day seminars to learn what it is and how to use it.

And when I looked into Activity Based Costing – heck, it was my old friend, Transactional Cost Analysis. Hello, Milk Truck Model.

All-day seminars! Are they kidding? I can explain the whole thing in ten minutes. In fact, here's my original article, *Planning for Profit on Smaller Orders* ...

Most companies set a minimum acceptable order level. Managers know, intuitively, that below some dollar amount an order is simply not profitable. But, too often, managers set their minimum order level too low, thus depressing profit.

Managers set order levels too low for a couple of reasons. First, they dislike turning away orders, even small orders. Second, and more significant, they lack techniques for analyzing profit for individual orders. Thus, they remain unaware of the extent to which smaller orders erode profit.

Unfortunately, conventional accounting techniques, while essential for reporting, provide poor tools for analyzing profit by order size. Using conventional techniques, managers allocate expenses either by direct-labor hours or by dollar sales. They should, instead, allocate a portion of expenses by order. That is, they should allocate certain expenses equally against each order regardless of order size.

Why? Let's consider a simple example – a company manufacturing electronics equipment on a "per-order" basis. It costs about as much to "set up" production for a fifty-piece order as for a one hundred piece order of the same product. That set-up cost is a per-order expense that remains substantially the same regardless of order size. Other per-order expenses include pulling parts from stock, issuing assembly instructions and setting up production equipment.

Look at the manufacturing company's Income Statement. Suppose, during the year, the firm sells $1,000,000 worth of equipment. Also, suppose that cost-of-goods-sold (cost of parts and materials, direct labor and factory overhead) totals $600,000, or 60% of sales. That leaves a gross profit of $400,000, or 40% of sales.

			% of Sales
Sales		$ 1,000,000	100 %
Cost of Goods Sold		600,000	60 %
Gross Profit		$ 400,000	40 %
Expenses			
Sales Expenses	$ 50,000		
Sales Commission Expenses	50,000		
Production Engineering Expenses	30,000		
R & D Expenses	20,000		
General & Admin. Expenses	150,000		
Total Expenses		300,000	30 %
Net Profit		100,000	10 %

Figure 20 - 1: Manufacturing Company's Year-End Income Statement

To determine net profit, subtract expenses from gross profit. Expenses are funds spent, not on producing products, but designing, marketing and selling products and managing the business.

These expenses include sales expense ($50,000), sales commissions expense ($50,000), production engineering expense ($30,000), research and development expense ($20,000) and general and administrative expense ($150,000). Total expenses are $300,000, or 30% of sales. Subtracting total expenses from gross profit leaves a net profit of $100,000, or 10% of sales.

This conventional income statement, like any other tool, has its limitations. It reports, not individually, but cumulatively, all orders for the period. If we tried to use it to predict profit for individual orders, we'd find it seriously misleading. We'd erroneously conclude that any order, regardless of size, had associated expenses of 30% of sales. Also we'd conclude that each order offered a net profit of 10% of sales.

Clearly, this is wrong. We cannot use this conventional income statement to predict profit for individual orders. It is useless for that purpose because it fails to recognize per-order expenses, and fails to allocate those expenses by order.

To properly allocate per-order expenses, we'll need to know the total number of orders. Suppose that number is 200. Two hundred separate orders were required to sell $1,000,000 worth of equipment – an average of $5,000 per order.

Next, we'll need to identify those expenses to allocate by order. Which specific expenses are of a per-order nature? Clearly, sales expense is one. Sales expense remains about the same regardless of order size. The sales staff spends about as much time in selling a $1,000, a $2,000 or a $3,000 order. Thus, we'll allocate the $50,000 sales expense over 200 orders to obtain $250 per order. (See Figure 20 - 2.)

Also, we should allocate production engineering expense by order. This expense is associated with preparing documentation for releasing orders to production. As documentation requirements

Size of Order (Dollars)			$2,000	$5,000	$10,000	$20,000
Cost of Goods Sold			1,200	3,000	6,000	12,000
Gross Profit			800	2,000	4,000	8,000
Expenses						
Sales Expenses	($50,000)	200 orders	250	250	250	250
Prodn. Eng. Exp.	($30,000)	200 orders	150	150	150	150
Sales Comm.	($50,000)	$1MM sales	100	250	500	1,000
R & D Expenses	($20,000)	$1MM sales	40	100	200	400
Gen. & Admin.	($20,000)	200 orders	100	100	100	100
Gen. & Admin.	($130,000)	$1MM sales	260	650	1,300	2,600
Total Expenses			900	1,500	2,500	4,500
Net Profit (Dollars)			($100)	$500	$1,500	$3,500
Net Profit (as % of Sales)			(5%)	10%	15%	17.5%

**Figure 20 - 2: Manufacturing Company's Analysis
of Profit by Order Size**

are independent of order size, this expense is of a per-order nature. That's $30,000 divided by 200 orders, or $150 per order.

Clearly, some expenses are correctly allocated by the conventional method – by dollar sales. One such expense is sales commission expense. Obviously, the higher the dollar sale, the higher the sales commission. Thus, we allocate sales commissions of $50,000 over $1,000,000 sales – that's 5% of sales.

Another expense correctly allocated by dollar sales is research and development. This expense does not relate to individual orders. Rather, it is justified by, and thus more closely relates to sales volume. Allocating this expense by dollar sales, we find $20,000 divided by $1,000,000 sales equals 2% of sales.

Finally, we should allocate certain expenses partly by order and partly by dollar sales. General and administrative expense is of this type. Since the company manufactures its products on a per-order basis, it must purchase some parts and materials on a per-order basis. Those G&A expenses associated with per-order purchases we should, logically, allocate by order. Those G&A

expenses associated with activities independent of individual orders we should allocate by dollar sales.

Let's assume the company has $20,000 G&A expense to be allocated by order and $130,000 G&A expense to be allocated by dollar sales. Then G&A expense allocated by order is $20,000 divided by 200 orders. That's $100 per order. G&A expense allocated by dollar sales is $130,000 over $1,000,000, or 13% of sales.

We've now uncovered the relationship between profit and order size. Obviously, profit increases as order size increases. More surprising however, below the average size order, profit falls dramatically. In fact, a $2,000 order actually produces a 5% loss!

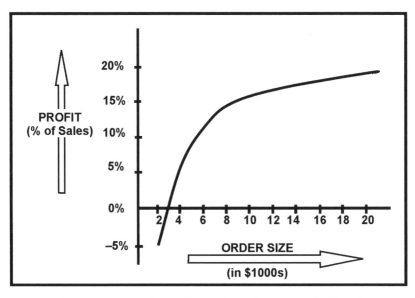

Figure 20 - 3: Manufacturing Company's Profit by Order Size

Now what? Having discovered that the company is losing money on its smaller orders, what strategy should its managers adopt? Should they simply increase the acceptable minimum order level?

Perhaps. However, this most obvious solution is but one available strategy. Another is to establish a finished goods inventory on more popular models. This would make production runs larger in size and, more significantly, smaller in number. This reduced number of production runs would, in turn, reduce both purchasing and production start-up expenses. Sales expense would, of course, remain unaffected.

Another strategy is to adjust sales price by size of order. This, in effect, establishes a "set-up" or "handling" charge in recognition of the per-order nature of certain expenses. For instance, a $300 set-up charge on a $2,000 order would convert a $100 net loss to a $200 net profit.

To some degree, per-order expenses are present in every business. For example, it requires about as much time, and thus money, to acknowledge a $1,000 order as a $2,000 order. To prepare the shipping papers. To type the invoice. To solve a customer's problem. To collect from a slow-paying account.

To determine profit by order size, identify per-order expenses and allocate those expenses by order. Knowing your profit by order size will enable you to make informed strategic decisions and, as a result, improve overall profit.

CHAPTER 21

BEWARE OF WALL STREET

A client company of mine is listed on the New York Stock Exchange. And though I wish it weren't so, the company's president spends more time with stock analysts than he does with his own vice-presidents. He works harder at promoting the price of the company's stock than he does managing the company's business. Why? Well, the traditional view of the business decision-making process is that it is totally rational – the "figuring out" of what to do based on an analysis of available alternatives.

There's good reason for this traditional view. For one, such rational decision-making is taught in our business schools. What MBA student hasn't had his or her share of decision trees, discounted cash flow and marginal cost analysis? And look at the business books both in academia and in your local book store. They're loaded with discussions on market position, effective advertising and the formula for calculating internal rate of return.

And corporate pronouncements from the captains of industry, whether at trade associations, press conferences or dinner speeches, all support this traditional, logical, methodical, almost "scientific" method of operating the business.

All of this "science" gets reported in the business and popular press, of course. So we all get sold on the fact that the running of American business is very "business-like" indeed.

And to a large extent, it is business-like. At least it starts out as such. It starts out with a management team's decision to develop a new product, for example. A decision based on real, "business-like" facts. And the various departments within the organization may very well get about the business of developing that product. The R&D department moves ahead in its development efforts. The marketing department busily researches a number of market segments and develops the appropriate distribution channels. And the production department busily re-tools the manufacturing process to accommodate the new product.

And then a funny thing happens. About ten-thirty one morning, the telephone rings on the president's desk. As the company is listed on the New York Stock Exchange, this morning's call is from a fellow on Wall Street in New York. He works for a major stock brokerage firm. He's called a stock analyst. What he does for a living is to figure out which stocks investors should by, and which they should sell.

"How does he do that?" you ask. By watching the quarterly returns of a few dozen or so companies in an industry. Or perhaps he'll cover two industries. Or three.

What's that? You wonder how he can tell what a company's long-range prospects are by watching quarterly returns. Well, I wonder that, too. And it turns out he really can't. All he can tell is what a firm's quarter-to-quarter financial performance *has been*. And since he's only a couple of years out of business school, and this is his first job, and he's never worked in any of the industries he's "specializing" in, he doesn't have a whole lot more to go by.

So, from time to time, he calls company presidents on the phone and asks questions such as, "How come your profits have been declining for the past two quarters?" And he listens carefully as the president explains, "We're investing in the future by developing a significant new product, and penetrating an important new market." Remember? Playing the game, not the shot.

And then the young analyst asks, "When will your company's earnings go back up?" and he listens politely as the CEO explains, "The company's long-term strategy is part of a three-year plan. And not until the third year of that plan will the investment begin to pay off. But when it does, the return on that investment will be quite significant."

Then the young analyst explains, "Three years is an awfully long time to expect an outside investor to hold any particular stock. Maybe the investors should think about selling the company's stock. Then buying it back in three years when the new product is ready to pay back on the long-term investment. I might recommend my investors sell the company's stock, unless ... unless you can figure out how to implement the new product strategy without impacting quarter-to-quarter earnings. Sure would be nice if you could do that," he continues, "because you do have an obligation to your shareholders. Got to support the price of our stock. You own quite a bit of stock in the company, too, as I recall."

Well, now the pressure is on. The president hurries over to the R&D department and asks the director of engineering if it isn't just possible to invent the same product using a third less capital. Then the president rushes to the marketing department to ask if it's possible to penetrate the intended market segment without benefit of an advertising budget. Then the president visits the manufacturing manager to ask if the production line really needs to be automated. One call, perhaps two, from the young analyst on Wall Street, and the company's long-term strategy, if not dead and buried, is seriously compromised.

Oh yes, you'll want to know the worst part of all. One of the firm's major competitors is located in China. And that competitor doesn't seem to be short-term focused at all. In fact, that competitor has been making significant investments in capital equipment to automate its own production line. And that capital equipment won't even pay back in three years, but will probably require more like seven, or eight, or even ten. But no one's really sure how long until payback, because the Chinese competitor didn't even make a payback calculation. He just believes that automation is the correct strategy. So he's made the investment.

And the Chinese bank that invested in that company isn't particularly concerned with the short term either. That bank views its investment as fairly long term. Ten years, twenty, or longer. Perhaps forever.

And yet another competitor, this one in the United States, is also making a long-term investment. That other competitor, a smaller company, is privately owned and operated. And while that smaller competitor hasn't nearly as much capital, its owner-managers have been able to focus on the longer term because they have no outside investors to satisfy. And their owner-managers understand that, by successfully implementing the right long-term strategies, they can create personal wealth. And they've got more than a few quarters to do that.

So the company whose stock is publicly traded is at a significant disadvantage to those competitors, both foreign and domestic, who have the luxury of making longer-term investments. Unless … unless the president of the publicly traded company has the guts to hang up on the young analyst from Wall Street.

DEVELOPING YOUR MISSION STATEMENT

Among attendees at our workshops, visitors to our web site and readers of our *Business Strategies Newsletter*, more managers ask about the mission statement than any other element in the strategic planning process. Their specific questions include: "What is a mission statement?" "Why do we need it?" and "How should we write it?"

A mission statement is a short, succinct statement declaring what business you're in and who your customer is. By offering this focus, it provides direction for future business development.

In 1960, Theodore Levitt wrote a historic article in *The Harvard Business Review*. In his article, "Marketing Myopia," Levitt criticized American business managers who, he claimed, define their business from the inside out. That is, American business managers focus on the products and services they provide – the nuts and bolts of their business – which, suggested Levitt, is a serious mistake.

To illustrate his point, Levitt claimed that the railroad industry caused its own decline by insisting that, "We're in the railroad business."

That statement led the railroad companies to think in terms of great hunks of iron and steel, rights-of-way a quarter of a mile wide across the United States, and large quantities of coal shipped across the Great Lakes. As they thought in terms of these physical factors, and insisted, "We're in the railroad business," they missed opportunities to participate in the growth segments of the transportation industry – in automobiles, in trucks, in airplanes.

According to Levitt, if the railroad companies had said, "We're in the transportation business," they might have fared much better. How come?

Because the railroad industry's customers don't care about great hunks of iron and steel. They don't care about rights-of-way across the country. They don't care about great quantities of coal. They simply care about moving people and products from one place to another. The market need that the railroads serve is transportation, not railroading.

The decline in the railroad industry came with the automobile and the airplane, each of which provided an alternative mode of transportation. Had the railroad companies recognized their mission as transportation, they might then have participated in one or both of those alternatives.

Two Sides to the Story

Certainly, Levitt has a point. But there's another point, too. The railroad industry happened to own the rights of way across the United States. And they owned the tracks. And they owned the iron and steel. All their assets had to do with the railroad industry. So there really are two sides to this story.

What if you wrote a statement linking these two points of view? Let's call that statement a mission statement. And you'll be sure to include two dimensions in that mission statement. The first dimension is an inside-out description of what you do. It will describe the product or service you supply and the activities you perform inside the walls of your company.

The second dimension of that statement is the "who buys it, and why" market-sided point of view.

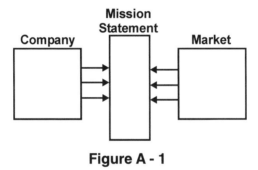

Figure A - 1

An Example

"Clayton Instruments, Inc. designs and manufactures highly reliable monitoring equipment to meet harsh or unusual environments within the process industries."

Consider the first half of Clayton's mission statement: *"Clayton Instruments, Inc. designs and manufactures highly reliable monitoring equipment ..."*

It's an inside-out description of what the company does. It lists the functional activities performed: *"design and manufacture."* And it describes the products that Clayton ships to its customers: *"highly reliable monitoring equipment."*

Consider the second half of Clayton's mission statement: *"... to meet harsh or unusual environments within the process industries."*

It describes the "Who buys it and why?" It's the market-sided definition of Clayton's business.

A well-developed mission statement is broad enough to allow for the diversity that management intends. And it also provides the focus to accurately describe what products and services the company offers.

Continuing with our Clayton Instruments example, though the company might currently manufacture temperature and pressure monitors only, its mission statement describes the firm's products more broadly. It speaks of monitoring equipment. This leaves room for the company's introduction of equipment other than temperature and pressure monitors. Thus the mission statement allows room for product expansion.

At the same time, the mission statement provides focus. It identifies the company's market as the process industries. And it specifically targets applications in *"harsh or unusual environments."*

Also, the word *"monitoring"* provides additional focus. Clayton Instruments does not manufacture data storage equipment. It does not manufacture control equipment. The company manufactures monitoring equipment and consciously eliminates other products. Presumably, the company's managers have explored their position in the industry and concluded that their expertise is in monitoring.

Evolution of Your Mission Statement

Managers often ask, "How much change might we expect in our mission statement from year to year?"

Expect very little change from year to year. Change in your mission statement is evolutionary rather than revolutionary. That's because your mission statement presents a foundation for what your company is, what it does, for whom, and why. As the foundation of your business – your link to your customers – you wouldn't want it to change very much from year to year.

Think of your mission statement as you would the Constitution of the United States. We *can* change the Constitution but not by very much. And we can't change it quickly. Same with your mission statement.

A number of companies (including a few of our clients) add one more element to their mission statement – a reference to "earning a profit" or "providing a return on stockholder equity."

This gives the mission statement a secondary purpose. Its primary purpose, of course, is to relate the organization to its market … to its customers. Adding "for a profit" to the mission statement relates the company to its stockholders. This can be helpful in getting the board of directors to approve the strategic plan of which the mission statement is a part.

How to Develop Your Mission Statement

A visitor to our website asked, "Is there some particular process you'd recommend my planning team use to develop our mission statement?"

Yes there is. First, have each member of your planning team independently write a mission statement for your organization. Then, have each person read their statement aloud to the others.

Next, take a large piece of paper – a flip-chart easel works great – and divide the page into four quadrants by drawing both a horizontal and a vertical line mid-way across, and mid-way down, the page. Head the four quadrants: "Product/Service," "Function," "Market," and "Market Position." (See Figure A - 2.)

Product/ Service	Market
Function	Market Position

Figure A - 2

Ask your planning team members, once again, to read the mission statements they've written. As they read, write the specific elements of each mission statement in the chart's corresponding quadrant. When they're finished reading – and you're finished writing – your chart will contain a handful of ways to describe your products and services, a handful of ways to describe your market, etc.

Now you can tackle one quadrant at a time. Have your planning team decide how best to describe the company's products or services, its market, etc. In effect, you're separating the discussions of each of the four elements of your mission statement.

Following your group's decision to adopt certain words and eliminate others for each of the four quadrants, you'll have most of the words in each quadrant crossed out, with just a few remaining. Next, ask each of your planning team members, once again, to write a mission statement. Except, this time, instruct them to use the words remaining on the chart.

As your planning team members each read their mission statements, you'll discover (to no one's surprise) that they're all quite similar. However, one or two will sound best, mainly because one or two individuals happen to have a flare for writing. Take the one or two which sound the best, copy them onto a clean sheet of paper (on the flipchart). After a little wordsmithing by your planning team, you've got your mission statement.

REINVENTING STRATEGIC PLANNING

The Strategy 21™ Process

It's time to reinvent the strategic planning process. Oh, don't get me wrong. I'm not suggesting that the traditional, tried and true strategic planning process doesn't work. For it does. In fact, I've successfully used the traditional process in my consulting work with clients for the last 24 years. It's just that, in today's "new economic reality" – the world of information technology, of networked organizations, of knowledge workers – the traditional process is a "force fit." Yes, I'll explain …

Let's first begin with a brief look at the traditional strategic planning process. (See Figure B – 1 on the next page.)

The traditional strategic planning process consists of four fundamental steps:
- Situation analyses
- Mission statement
- Objectives
- Strategies

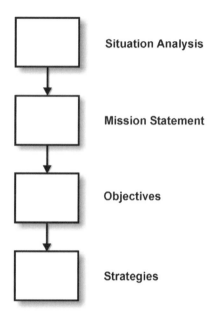

Figure B - 1: The Traditional Strategic Planning Process

The first step, *situation analysis*, includes a look at internal strengths and weaknesses as well as external opportunities and threats. Its purpose is to answer the question, "Where are we today?"

The *mission statement* declares what business the organization is in, who its customers are, and what specific benefit the organization provides to those customers. *Objectives*, of course, are quantified measurements of success. They address the question, "Where do we wish to arrive, and when?" As such, they characterize the management team's vision of the desired future state, and they are quantified so that the organization can measure its arrival at that state.

Finally, *strategies* are the activities that the organization will implement to achieve its objectives (the desired future state). As such, strategies answer the question, "How do we get from here to there?"

Unfortunately, there is one major problem with the traditional strategic planning process. It simply isn't suggestive of the timely strategic issues that the planning team must discuss. It doesn't demand that the planning team wrestle with the strategic issues of the 21st century. For example, it doesn't specifically recognize the significance of the knowledge worker individually, and of all knowledge workers collectively as a learning organization.

Also, it doesn't directly point the planning team's attention toward opportunities and threats outside of their current industry, such as threats from substitute products and services, or threats from new competitive entrants.

Yes, it is possible to overcome this deficiency in the traditional strategic planning process. But doing so requires not just a sharp mind for business, but also expertise in planning plus strong facilitation skills. Unfortunately, very few management teams possess this combination of expertise.

And so, we need a new process. One that lends itself to the issues of the "new economic reality." The realities of information technology, of learning organizations, of knowledge workers and empowered employees, and of networked enterprises. Ideally, this new process would be strongly suggestive of content. That is, the very titles of the process steps should direct the planning team toward the strategic issues they need discuss – the strategic issues of the 21st century.

And so, I propose a change. A reinvention of the strategic planning process to a new form of planning appropriate to the 21st century. I propose a process which we call Strategy 21™.

As the name implies, we've developed the process to focus on the critical issues of our 21st century. What are those issues? They're those fast changing drivers in our business lives that make all of us so terribly busy. That make our business environment, so very often, seem like chaos. They're the issues of the "new economic reality" – the world of information technology, of networked organizations, of global competition. And of the significance of the knowledge worker.

The new economic reality also includes significant opportunities and threats beyond the "traditional" set of competitors. Like threats from substitute products and services, or threats from new competitive entrants. As you know, threats from new competitors are especially dangerous as it is those new competitive entrants who, so often, can (and do) change "the rules of the game." Example: Dell Computer entered the industry with a brand new business model – a web-based custom ordering system – and thus redefined how computers would be sold profitably … much to the dismay of all of the "traditional" industry-insider competitors.

Using the Strategy 21™ Process

To use the Strategy 21™ Process, schedule a series of half-day to full-day sessions with your strategy team as follows (see Figure B – 2).

Examine the Organization's Current Business Model

During your first strategy session, conduct an examination of your current business model. Look at your business model from suppliers through customers. Draw a block diagram on a flipchart easel. Draw a box to represent each of the organizations involved in providing everything from raw material to finished product (or service) to your end customer. Discuss which of the various participants are adding value. Where, in the diagram, is that value generated? By whom? And how much?

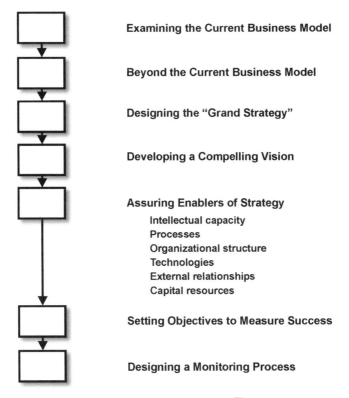

Examining the Current Business Model

Beyond the Current Business Model

Designing the "Grand Strategy"

Developing a Compelling Vision

Assuring Enablers of Strategy
 Intellectual capacity
 Processes
 Organizational structure
 Technologies
 External relationships
 Capital resources

Setting Objectives to Measure Success

Designing a Monitoring Process

Figure B - 2: The Strategy 21 ™ Process

Use the block diagram you've drawn to examine your competitive environment. Discuss what competitive advantage your organization enjoys? What provides you that advantage? Is your position of advantage stable? Why or why not? In what ways is your organization competitively deficient? What factors are making it so?

Discuss trends (both positive and negative) among markets, suppliers, competitors and regulators. What are the key issues in the marketplace? How are those issues likely to affect your business over the next few years?

Decide what core competencies have led to your success to date? How do these competencies translate to value for your customers? Are these competencies truly of competitive advantage?

Are they impossible – or at least extremely difficult – for your competitors to emulate? And why?

What are your "natural" constraints to growth? What's holding you back? What's the weakest link in your business model?

Scan the Environment Outside of Your Current Business Model – a look "outside the box."

At your second strategy retreat, look beyond your current business model. At the broader "macro-environment." The world beyond your firm, your customers and your competitors. At seemingly tangentially related issues, for the issues in the macro-environment aren't specific to your organization. They're not even specific to your industry but you'll need be aware of them because they have the potential – particularly in today's fast changing environment – to affect your company.

First, look to potential new competitors. Consider which companies currently provide similar products or services, but to a different set of customers. These companies represent a potential competitive threat.

And which companies currently sell, to your customers, some related product or service? Potentially, those companies might diversify their line to compete with you, thus presenting another threat from a new competitor.

Explore which products or services might represent a substitute to those which you're selling. Consider which of those potential substitutes might provide your customers with the same or similar benefits, or might fulfill the very same needs perhaps less expensively, more conveniently or more quickly.

Are there substitute modes of marketing and selling (e.g., the Internet) that your company, or a competitor's company, might employ? Is there a more cost-effective or convenient way for customers to purchase?

How about substitute modes of distribution? Again, are there more cost effective, or more convenient, ways to deliver product or service to customers.

Designing the "Grand Strategy" – three fundamental choices

After (1) examining the current business model, and (2) looking beyond the current business model, the third, step is to design the "grand strategy." This step will likely require more than a single strategy session. For it involves not only discussions among your strategy team, but a fair degree of reflective thought as well.

Designing the grand strategy is really about choosing. About choosing one of three possible options. As follows:

- Strategy #1 – Continue with your current business model only, i.e., doing business "the same old way" … only better.
- Strategy #2 – Change to a new business model, i.e., stop doing business the old way, and instead, conduct business in some new fashion.
- Strategy #3 – Diversify so as to manage multiple business models.

An example might be instructive. Let's consider the traditional supermarket where you likely do most of your food shopping. Were the managers of the grocery chain to meet for a strategy session, they might decide to continue to do business in the same traditional fashion. They'd continue to have huge regional warehouses from which large delivery trucks deliver the food items in the back door, they'd stock the shelves during the night-time hours, and sell retail out the front door through a self-serve / shopping cart process. Just as they do today.

Sure, they might decide to make some improvements to their business, but not to change it in any fundamental way. They'd then have elected the first strategy, i.e., to stay with the same business model.

On the other hand, a grocer – likely one who has not been dominant using the traditional grocery business model – might decide to switch to selling product over the Internet. Or by mail order catalog. Or though ads in health magazines. Or through food-buying coops. Electing any of these alternate business models would clearly be of major strategic change representative of Strategy #2. Clearly, an organization electing to make such change must carefully consider the associated challenges. For switching to a very different business model would require a very different set of managerial skills, a very different mix of resources, and a customer base willing to go along with the change.

Imagine next the managers from the same grocery chain deciding on choice #3 – to operate two business models simultaneously. Here they might decide to open a drive-up delivery window at the back door of their current supermarket operation. Yes, customers could still park their cars in front of the market, and walk through the front door pushing a grocery cart before them. Yes, those same customers could still unload their groceries onto the same traditional check-out counter.

But by electing Strategy #3, the managers would be offering their customers a second choice. That is, to call ahead (via an Internet website or cellular phone while driving home from work) to order their groceries, then drive up to the back door of the supermarket. Then, without ever turning off their engine, simply open the car's trunk so a supermarket employee could load the grocery order into the trunk of their car ... all paid for using a bank debit card.

Here again, the grocery's management team would need carefully consider the challenges to adding this additional business model. Not the least of which is the challenge to operations. For their drive-up window would require that the store's employees not only received the phone-in order, but also did the picking and packing. Higher labor content certainly. Would the marginal revenue received at the drive-up window pay for the additional labor? Or are the margins on grocery items just too low to support such service? Or might the customer be willing to pay a service charge for the added convenience of driving up and having groceries delivered into the trunk of the car? All these are questions which the strategy team must explore.

While choosing Strategy #3 – managing multiple business models – might seem especially risky, it's actually becoming more and more commonplace … because of the Internet. Many traditional, "retail store" companies now also run an on-line operation. In fact, Strategy #3 has become the "brick and mortar" company's answer to the dot.coms. Consider, for example, Barnes and Noble's Internet presence in response to Amazon.com.

Building Emotional Energy – developing a compelling vision

Once having decided on its grand strategy, your team needs to begin building the organization's emotional energy. This means getting everyone in your company excited about the strategy and excited about its successful implementation.

The strategy team needs to develop a compelling vision of the future. A vision that your employees will enthusiastic embrace – because the vision is worthy, and because it challenges them to grow. Considering the drive-up window at the grocery store, for example, the vision might be one of "Saving time for the busy shoppers of the world." The grocery chain might actually calculate (in fact, they've probably already calculated) how many hours the grocery shoppers of the Western World spend pushing carts up and down the aisle. See? A big vision!

In order for you to get your employees passionate about your vision, it must be compelling. It must matter, not just to your management team, but also to your employees. "To triple sales revenue next year" doesn't do it. Who cares? Certainly not minimum wage shelf-stockers. To make a difference to customers, the community, the world, or to improve the lives of human beings … that matters.

Interestingly, a vision doesn't have to be grounded in today's reality. It simply has to project a compelling story about the future. When Steve Jobs said, "An Apple on every desk," well heck, there wasn't then an Apple on every desk. In fact, there won't *ever* be an Apple on every desk. That's OK. You can think of the vision figuratively, rather than a literally.

It's also important for management not just to speak the vision, but also to *live* the vision. Apple Computer did this. Did you know that the entire design team for the Apple II GS computer signed their name on the artwork for the computer's mother board? So on each and every Apple II GS computer, the team's signatures appear in copper script. Now *that's* involving employees in living the vision.

Your team needs to decide how it will communicate its vision to your employees, how to continue to nurture and support that vision every day, in every way, and how to empower employees to fulfill that vision.

Assuring Enablers and Tracking Success

Once having decided on your grand strategy, and having developed your compelling vision for that grand strategy, your planning team will need satisfy itself that your organization has, or can obtain, all of the resources necessary to enable that strategy. This step of assuring necessary resources is a great place to involve a selection of mid-level managers, both for their input and to build their commitment toward the successful implementation of the strategy. (Refer to Figure B – 2 on page 193.)

Enabler #1: Intellectual Capacity – creating a learning organization

The discussion on intellectual capacity might well parallel our earlier discussion on "Building Knowledge in Your Organization" (see Chapter 12). Again, the object is to encourage people to learn and grow together. Thus, your strategy team should discuss developing an on-going process to capture and share collective knowledge (see "Steps Required," in Chapter 12).

You'll also need face an especially tough question: Do you have the "right" people? If not, what changes should you make? Changes in people? In your hiring and retaining processes?

Consider this: In today's information economy, people are, indeed, your most valuable asset. The knowledge worker carries the very success of the enterprise around in his head. With power having so moved to the employee, the knowledge worker is relatively free to pick up and move, to decide that the next organization down the road is more worthy of his efforts.

That puts the employer in a position of having to compete for the talents and the buy-in of the knowledge worker. And it also makes the employer more vulnerable, not only to individual knowledge workers leaving, but also to adverse cultural changes due to knowledge workers not working together as a team.

For these reasons, it's imperative that the organization hire the "right" people, individuals who not only offer the requisite knowledge and skills, but will also "fit right" with the culture. Hiring the wrong person is loaded with hidden expenses of trying to fit a square peg into a round hole. It just won't work. And, in the end, it will be terribly costly. As Mark Twain said, "Never try to teach a pig to sing. You'll fail to do it, and you'll annoy the pig." Well, today's competitive environment is unforgiving of wasting time trying to teach a pig to sing – or wasting time with any other such impossible task. If you want singing, hire a canary, not a pig. You need to spend your valuable time running your business, so hire the right people in the first place and your life will be easier.

I always worry when I see a company prepared to compromise because the right person is hard to find, so in desperation they hire "a warm body." Such hiring in desperation may well make managers feel better in the short term, but it's darn near a sure bet they'll soon regret having done so.

Enabler #2: Processes

Next, consider the processes necessary to your chosen strategy? Do you currently have those processes in place? If not, how will you build those processes? And when? Returning to the grocery chain example, the addition of a drive-up window would call for many additional processes, such as order receipt, picking, packing, payment processing and delivery.

Certainly those mid-level managers expert in such operations would be meaningful additions to the strategy team during the discussions regarding processes.

Enabler #3: Organizational Structure

Questions regarding organizational structure come next. You'll need to address whether your organizational structure is correct for your chosen strategy? If not, what preferred structure should replace it? And how should you transition into that preferred organizational structure? And when can you begin such transition?

Imagine the transition from traditional retail grocery store to mail order catalog grocer. Quite a significant change, requiring new skill sets such as catalog design and direct mail sales.

Enabler #4: Technologies

Here in our 21st century, technology plays a major role in all businesses. So your strategy team needs to wrestle with the question of which technologies are necessary to enable your chosen strategy. Do you currently possess expertise in those chosen technologies? If not, how will you obtain that expertise? And when?

Depending on your management team's expertise in the applicable technologies, it may be beneficial to include an outside expert in your discussions. Not to make strategic decisions for your planning team, but rather to offer information and recommendations regarding applicable technologies.

Enabler #5: External Relationships

Consider next what external relationships are necessary to enable your chosen strategy? The grocer's drive-up window requires the services of a phone company. Selling groceries by direct mail catalog requires the services of United Parcel Service and, potentially, an order fulfillment / warehousing company.

Do you currently have the necessary external relationships? If so, what can you do to enhance them? And if not, how can you establish them? With whom? And when?

Enabler #6: Capital Resources

Consider, too, the necessary capital resources. Discuss whether you have the funds to enable your chosen strategy? If not, how can you obtain those funds? And when? Clearly, managers from your finance department would be helpful additions to these discussions.

Setting Quantified Objectives – deciding how to measure success

Objectives are your indicators of success. They therefore describe your "desired future state."

Categories of Objectives

When developing objectives, consider six categories:
1. Financial
2. Marketing/Sales
3. Products/Services
4. Operations
5. Human Resources
6. Community.

Within each of these six categories, you can select from a number of specific measurements for an objective. For example, your financial objective might measure profitability in any of its various flavors, such as gross profit, operating profit, or net profit, either before or after tax. Or you can write your financial objective in terms of return on assets, return on investment, or cash on hand.

Marketing or sales objectives measure "how much or how many?" You might set this objective in terms of sales volume, sales growth rate, market share or number of market segments effectively served.

Your products / services objective might quantify the quality of products or services, new products and services introduced, or customer satisfaction. And your operational objective might measure efficiency, productivity or cost reduction.

Your objective dealing with human resources – the people side of the business – can measure employee benefits, employee satisfaction, employee training or employee turnover.

Finally, your social objective – your non-economic or community-related objective – might deal with the non-pollution of air and water, equal opportunity employment, or being a good corporate citizen.

If you will benefit from developing more than one objective in a particular category, then do it. For example, you may write an objective for total sales, another for sales of a particular product line, and a third for sales to a specific market segment.

Caution though. Be careful not to set too many objectives. If you do, you'll lose focus. You won't be able to use your objectives in managing day-to-day. Consider this: If you can't memorize your objectives, you've probably got too many. For the memories of most of us, that's about six. Remember the CEO on the camel race across Australia and his one-minute phone call (chapter 3).

Criteria of Objectives

Be sure to quantify your objectives. For you must be able to measure each one and to figure out whether or not you've successfully accomplished it. More importantly, everyone in your organization must know how hard to "push" to achieve it.

Sometimes it's easy to quantify an objective. Sometimes it's not. It all depends on the category of the objective. Financial objectives are the easiest to quantify. After all, the world of finance is numbers on pieces of paper. And marketing objectives are usually easy enough to turn into numbers. Certainly you can quantify sales volume.

But how about something like customer satisfaction? A pretty gray area, isn't it? Some say customer satisfaction is so difficult to quantify, that you can't do it. Or can you?

Sure you can! You can count complaints. You can measure defective products returned for replacement. You can count referrals to new accounts. Or repeat business. Or warranty cost.

So customer satisfaction will be where you want it when warranty cost falls below 1.5%; or when repeat business rises to over 75%; or when referrals to new accounts reach 25% of total billings. The point is, figure out a way to quantify each of your objectives.

Also, make sure that each of your objectives is both challenging and, at the same time, attainable. People in your organization should understand that accomplishment of the objective requires that they "stretch." But given that stretch, they should expect they can accomplish the objective. That the objective is achievable.

The analogy I like is the basketball hoop. The hoop is ten feet above the floor of the gymnasium. At that ten foot level, the game is both challenging and also attainable. If the hoop were four feet above the floor of the gymnasium, it wouldn't be challenging and your players wouldn't need to work very hard at playing the game.

If the hoop were a hundred and four feet above the floor of the gymnasium, it wouldn't be attainable, so your players wouldn't work very hard at playing the game. It's your job to keep your players working hard at playing the game. You must find that "ten foot level" for each objective. Make each of your objectives both challenging and attainable.

Once a challenging objective has been reached, you can maybe "raise the hoop a little." Until runner Roger Bannister achieved a four-minute mile on May 6, 1954, everyone thought that the feat was unattainable, but once he'd done the undoable, many more runners followed with their own sub-four-minute mile.

Assuring Implementation – designing a monitoring process

A monitoring process will help you track the implementation of your strategy, thus the accomplishment of your objectives – the arrival at your desired future state.

Most strategy teams decide to monitor their strategy through a process of periodic review, generally a quarterly review. And, in fact, for a multi-year strategic plan, a quarterly review seems about right. Remember though, those responsible for implementing any particular strategy will also conduct a more detailed, more tactical review. In effect, the review process continues on two levels – both strategic and tactical.

At each quarterly review session, your strategy team should meet to review the "variables." Those variables are objectives and strategy. You'll need to track both. You'll track your strategy to determine if you're implementing it according to your earlier intentions. You'll track your objectives to determine if (through the implementation of the strategy), you're accomplishing what matters most – the fulfillment of your objectives.

Each year, at the last of your quarterly review sessions, save some time for one additional discussion. That of the process itself. Ask any and all questions regarding what's worked, what hasn't, and how you might alter the strategy process to make it work still better. Ask for suggestions regarding the timing of your strategy sessions. Ask about format, about agenda, about selection of participants, and about discussion topics.

Most importantly, ask if your strategy process is nurturing strategic thinking. If the members of your strategy team are successfully communicating their strategic vision throughout your organization. And if that strategic vision, the building of knowledge among your employees, and the successful implementation of your strategy, are enabling your organization to pull ahead of your competition in the challenging environment of our 21st century.

Index

Visit Bill Birnbaum's Web Site at:
www.BirnbaumAssociates.com

There you'll find insightful articles on strategic thinking, strategic planning and strategy implementation.

Articles on the web site include such topics as:

- Is your management team ready to think strategically?
- Why strategic thinking must lead strategic planning – *never* the other way around
- Questions to ask when selecting your strategy consultant
- Key success factors in strategic planning
- Common planning mistakes and how to avoid them
- Break free from that same old "rote planning process"
- Is this year's strategy simply last year's strategy "warmed over"?
- Strategic thinking: tools and techniques
- Strategy implementation: Six supporting factors
- The action plan – your key to successful strategy implementation

Also on the web site, you'll find information about the services which Bill Birnbaum provides to his client companies.

Visit Bill Birnbaum's web site at:
www.BirnbaumAssociates.com

A quote from Bill Birnbaum:

"My personal objective for any strategy session is that my client's management team thinks more strategically about their enterprise than they *ever* have before."